What Does Your Brain Need?

Everything You Need to Know About Your Brain Health: Memory Improvement Techniques, Habits For Brain and Creativity, Brain Reset

By Andrew Stinson

Table of Contents

Introduction

"Life isn't about finding yourself. Life is about creating yourself."

~ George Bernard Shaw

Your wisdom lies in investing time and effort in your self-growth. Your likes and dislikes reveal that your mind controls and decides your approach towards people, incidents, and experiences.

You often wonder why success comes so easily to certain people. The answer is, successful people make optimum use of their brainpower. Let us dwell deep to discover the incredible power of the brain, access its untapped reservoir to create a happy, and fulfilled life. It is a journey from mediocrity to all-round excellence. So, are you ready to receive the tried and tested ways to experience abundance, multiply your happiness manifold in every situation, and escape the misery and suffering forever?

The SHORTEST and SUREST Path to Getting Everything You Want in Life is by preparing your mind to work for you with its full potential in a unique, authentic and compelling manner, and let the Universe do the rest for you.

Chapter 1: Knowing Your Brain

Human Brain Facts, Functions and Anatomy

The human brain is considered to be the most complicated organ in the animal kingdom. It has more than 10 billion neurons. The human brain carries out all higher mental functions. It is the seat of thinking, memory, reasoning, perception, emotions, mental abilities, and speech. The brain weighs approximately 1400 grams. Unlike other tissues, the brain is solely dependent on glucose for its energy requirements. It uses 20% of the total oxygen consumed by the body. It is, however, shocking that we know very little about the way it functions. For example, we do not know much about memory, and we do not know why we can learn and remember only some information more easily.

Inside the Human Brain: A tour of how the mind works

Your Brain is: Three Pounds, Three Parts

Your brain is your most important, complicated, and powerful organ. Your brain receives countless messages from different parts of the body. It processes them, and then sends prompt instructions to them. You will be surprised to know that your brain weighs only about three pounds. It has a texture similar to a firm jelly. The human brain resembles a walnut. Your brain is made up of several millions of nerve cells and nerve fibers. Externally, it is protected by the skull; which protects it from shocks, jerks, and bumps. There is a fluid between the skull and the brain. The fluid acts as a shock absorber and protects the delicate brain from injuries.

Cerebrum (Forebrain), Cerebellum (Hindbrain), and Medulla (Brain stem) are the three parts of the human brain. Each part performs a specific role.

Cerebrum (Forebrain)

This is the upper part of the brain. It is dome-shaped, and the largest part of the brain. The cerebrum fills up most of your skull and takes up 80 percent of your brain, and sits upfront and center. It controls your thinking, remembering, problem-solving, feeling, and movement.

The primary functions of the cerebrum:

- Interprets sensations, such as hearing, vision, smell, and vision

- Controls your emotions and feelings

- Thinking, problem-solving, and adapting our behaviors

- Remembering and learning

- Using and understanding language to communicate

- Interpreting things around us

- Body movement

It is divided symmetrically into two hemispheres- left hemisphere and right hemisphere. The right hemisphere controls the left side of the body and vice versa. Thus, when one side of the brain gets damaged, the opposite side of the body is affected. The nerve fibers, through which cerebrum communicate with each other, is called white matter. The large white matter in the cerebrum is called the corpus callosum. It connects the two hemispheres.

Cerebrum comprises of nerve cells responsible for thinking, reasoning, controlling memory, thoughts, intelligence and learning, and also controls the sense organs. This part is larger in humans relative to body size in any other vertebrates because humans are considered more intelligent than any other vertebrate.

Lobes of the Cerebrum

Each lobe is divided based on the specific function it serves. Very complex relationships exist between the lobes of the brain, and also between the left and right hemispheres.

The primary functions of each lobe of the cerebrum include:

- The frontal lobes, which are the biggest, are located upfront. They're the "executive" part of the brain. All the higher-order thinking happens here, including planning, organizing, reasoning, adapting your behavior to fit the given environment or situation. They also control speech, movement, and, to some extent, your emotion.

- The parietal lobes are situated right behind the frontal lobes. They are primarily responsible for receiving, recognizing, and interpreting sensory information, such as taste, smell, temperature, and touch from the outside world. They help you to understand spatial relationships, like size, shape, and the orientation of objects about your body. This area is also vital for reading, solving mathematical problems, and other academic skills.

- The temporal lobes are located right above the ears and help us process the sound and noise we hear, including music. They are involved in memory, learning, and the understanding of language.

- The occipital lobes at the back of the brain help to interpret the things you see.

Cerebellum (Hindbrain)

The cerebellum is located towards the back of the brain and is the part tucked away under the cerebrum. It is much smaller than the cerebrum. It is about 11 percent of your brain and packed with neurons. This works under the control of the cerebrum. It coordinates the working of our muscles and also helps us in maintaining our balance. Athletes must have proper muscular coordination to win a race. If you observe a typist or a pianist at work, you will realize how the muscles of the hands work as a team in proper coordination. The Cerebellum does all these coordinations.

The functions of the cerebellum include:

- Learning
- Coordinating movement and balance
- Fine-tunes your thoughts, emotions, touch, smell, and other senses

The cerebellum helps you to "automate" movements. It helps you to do things like, learn dance moves, and type quickly and accurately.

Medulla (Brainstem)

The medulla is a stem-shaped structure. The medulla controls all the involuntary activities such as breathing, heartbeat, and blood circulation. It works even when you sleep. The brainstem connects 11 other cranial nerves in the head. The brain stem controls automatic functions, which are essential to maintaining life:

- Breathing
- Heart rate and blood pressure
- Digestion
- Body temperature
- Reticular activating system (RAS) that makes the brain alert (in conjunction with the thalamus, hypothalamus, and cerebellum)

Supply Lines:

Your body's most vibrant networks of blood vessels provide your brain its nourishment. Your brain tends to use up to 50 percent of oxygen and fuel when you are thinking intensely.

The whole nerve vessel network comprises of arteries, veins, and capillaries.

The Cortex: "Thinking Wrinkles:

This part of your brain is actively involved in

- Processing Sights
- Processing Sounds
- Processing Smells
- Thoughts, Problem Solving & Planning
- Controlling Voluntary Movement

Left Brain and Right Brain:

The brain is divided into two halves, the left half and the right half. Even to date, experts are not sure how and why the "right-brain" and the "left-brain" differ in function. In most of us, the left-brain has a language area. It is interesting to note that the right-brain controls the movement on your body's left side and vice versa.

The Neuron Forest:

An adult human brain contains approximately 100 billion nerve cells. The nerve branches connect the nerve cells at more than 100 trillion points. This dense, scientists call the branching network a "neuron forest." In Alzheimer's disease, neurons are destroyed.

Cell Signaling:

Your brain is a complicated machine, and the real work goes on in its cells. The neurotransmitters in your brain carry signals to the other cells traveling across the synapse.

Scientists have identified the presence of dozens of such neurotransmitters. Alzheimer's disease disrupts both the activity of neurotransmitters and the way electrical charges travel within cells. Each nerve cell connects to another nerve cell at synapses.

Signal Coding:

Your brain's raw material is billion nerve cells, 100 trillion synapses, and dozens of neurotransmitters. Over some time, your regular experiences create definite patterns in the signal type and signal strength. It is through these patterns of activity that, at the basic cellular level, your brain codes your thoughts, memories, expectations, emotions, skills, and the sense of who you are.

Chapter 2: The Importance of Your Brain

"Why do human beings need a brain?"

Though this appears to be a silly question, the answer we commonly get is 'to stay alive.' Indeed, this is true. The brain receives information through your five senses, namely sight, smell, touch, taste, and hearing - often many at one time. Your brain assembles all these messages and makes it meaningful for you. At the same time, it is stored in your memory. Hence, your brain controls your memory, thoughts, movement, and speech. You would be dead without your brain, which is why "brain dead" is usually the common medical and the legal definition of death. However, the brain is not solely responsible for staying alive. The other primary organs, including liver, heart, and lungs, are also responsible for it. We can indeed transplant any of the human organs, but not the brain.

Brainless Species:

Amazingly, there are many animals on this earth without a brain. They only have a simple nervous system, for example, sea squirt. This creature once it implants into a rock, the first thing it does is it eats its brain and nervous system because when there is no need to move, you don't need the neurons. Humans have brain to facilitate attention, emotions, empirical processes and produce adaptable and complex movements.

The primary purpose of the brain is to allow human beings to live meaningfully. It is a myth that bigger brains are more intelligent because it will have more brain cells. It is not fully true. The number of neurons does not determine the intelligence, but the number of connections between the neurons does.

It is most interesting to watch one's mind. When your mind is not trained and taught, it will get lost in all stories, notions, beliefs, and issues. So, you have to train our mind to work optimally for you.

Brain Facts You Must Know:

- The brain of an adult weighs about 3 pounds.

- Approximately 75 percent of your brain is made up of water. Hence, the dehydration in small amounts also harms brain functions.

- The human brain grows three times its size in the first year. It continues to grow until you are 18 years old.

- A chemical reaction in the brain combined with the muscles and nerves of your head and neck causes the headaches.

- The human brain is made up of approximately one hundred billion neurons.

- The key to learning and memory is Cholesterol. But high cholesterol has adverse effects depending on your age and other factors.

- Though brain interprets pain signals sent to it, it cannot feel the pain.

- The human brain starts to lose memory abilities and some cognitive skills by late 20s.

- Human brain gets smaller as we get older.

- Many of us heard saying that a human being uses only 10 percent of the brain. But it is not true. We use all of our brains.

- For all activities like sight, smell, touch, etc. neurons carry messages from the brain to other organs and vice-versa too. The information is carried at different speeds. The highest speed at which information passes between neurons is about 250 mph.

- Dreams which we see in sleep are the combination of imagination, neurological factors, and psychological factors. It is proof that your brain works even while sleeping also.

- Phantom limb pain syndrome is when the central nervous system, which includes your brain, continues to feel the pain of an amputated limb.

- Sphenopalatine ganglion neuralgia happens when you eat or drink something cold. It freezes the arteries and blood vessels that are present in the very back of the throat, including the ones that take blood to your brain. Sometimes, this causes the pain in your forehead as the nerves get constrict when they are cold and open back when they are warm again.

- Egyptians usually remove the brain through the nose during the mummification.

- Impact of alcohol on the brain is blurred vision, unsteady walk, and slurred speaking. However, prolonged consumption of alcohol can affect the brain permanently and cannot reverse once you become sober. Long term effects of alcohol consumption include memory issues and reduced cognitive function.

- Traumatic events can also affect the brain's ability to remember details.

- Though Computer or some video games are thought to help improve cognitive abilities, however, more studies must be conducted to learn how much they help, or what types of games help.

- You may lose consciousness if blood supply to the brain is cut off for more than 8 to 10 seconds.

- The Human brain can survive only for 4 to 6 minutes without oxygen.

- It can generate 10 to 23 watts of energy in waking.

- The blood vessels present in the brain are nearly 100,000 miles in length.

Chapter 3: How The Brain Works

Most of the time, we live merely with our thoughts. Sometimes, we may be entertaining other's thoughts by reading a book, watching a movie, talking with people, or listening to audio. However, mostly, we hear our own "voice" or "thoughts." Thoughts are compelling, which affect and influence our behavior. Finally, it makes us what we are at the current point.

Storage Of Data In The Brain:

Memory:

The human mind is capable of anything. However, when we do not use it the right way, we tend to lose it. We can sharpen our memory through different techniques. A good memory is the best asset one can possess. An intelligent person has a razor-sharp memory, and will naturally succeed in all ventures.

Mirrors Neurons In The Brain:

In a study made in the mid-'90s, mirrors neurons were found in the brain of the macaque monkey. These neurons very actively fire both when the monkey was seeing the experimenter grasping an object, and when the monkey itself was doing the action. These neurons are present in the human brain too. The mirror neurons act when we act, and also when seeing others acting. So, it is better to have a disciplined and trained mind.

Trained mind Vs. Untrained mind:

A trained mind is well-structured, progressive, monitored, and regulated. Whereas, an untrained mind usually focuses on what one wants but lacks rather than on what one needs and has.

The first step to train our brain is constantly keeping a check of what you are thinking. Analyze your thoughts as an editor, editing a manuscript. Or, observe your thoughts as a monitor. Record your thoughts. Finally, you can start to regulate and train your brain. This practice helps to know your thinking. Unless we understand what is controlling our life, we cannot manage or regulate it.

One advantage of this practice is that we can avoid the thoughts about which we have already finished thinking. It wastes our time and takes up "space" in the brain. Instead of this, we can have new thoughts.

Thinking about the same thing, again and again, is like reading the same book, the same phrases, the same stories over and over, and nothing new.

However, there are some exceptions like principles or truth may be reminded again and again, or a thought which makes me happy can be rethought, etc. We should always feed our brain with new thoughts so that it is filled with joy and happiness. We need to engage in discussion with knowledgeable people to come into contact with new thoughts. But you should avoid replaying the same thoughts that could pamper unhealthy messages to produce mental and emotional illness like anxiety, suspicion, insecurity, pride, etc.

Though the neuroscience has progressed dramatically over the last few decades, the understanding of how the human brain works is not clear yet. The human brain is responsible for memorizing things, processing data, and acting on the data. Most of the information our brain receives will be visual. In the 1950s and 1960s, it was discovered that long-term memories are stored not in one part of the brain, but distributed widely throughout the cortex. Memory storage is, in fact, an ongoing process of uninterrupted reclassification from the continuous changes in neural pathways, and the parallel processing of information in the human brain.

This Is How Your Memory Works:

Memory is formed depending on the attention paid to the information and the usefulness of the information received. There is a vast network of neurons that communicate with each other across synapses. If this network and synapses are robust, then the information is better maintained. This is a memory.

We don't have a separate storage unit in the brain. The memory is just stored all over the brain.

Different Forms Of Memory:

Short-term memory:

Short-term memory processes the sensory memories, which are more interesting to us. The short-term memory has limited capacity. So, by repeating it again and again, it may be stored in short-term memory for a longer period, i.e. up to a few hours. The capacity of short-term memory can be increased by a process known as "chunking." In this, we group items to form larger items. For example, to memorize a 12 digit phone number, we group the digits in pairs which gives six chunks to remember easily.

Long-term memory:

The long-term storage of memory of personal details, unique skills, life events, etc. Many times, the memories stored in our short-term memories can be forgotten quickly. Sometimes, it is a good thing. If we didn't forget the memories, then handling the huge volume of information that we come across daily will be very difficult. The human brain will be overloaded with information, and processing it meaningfully will become impossible.

To store more memories, we need to consciously take effort to transfer the information from short-term to long-term memory. For example, students revise the subjects many times before examinations; the systematic repetition of affirmations to see the expected changes in our life or rehearsing the information enables to transfer the data to long-term memory. Sometimes, it is possible to store the information directly in the long-term memory. For example, we know that touching the switches in wet hands can cause shock. You don't need to experience the shock again and again to memorize that.

It is important to remember that many of the designs and visuals will not be stored in long-term memory. Only the conclusions and the summary will be transferred to long-term memory.

Sensory Memory:

The memories that originate from the sensory organs, such as the eyes or nose and stored only for a minimal amount of time is called Sensory Memory. It typically lasts only for 500 milliseconds. It is also known as iconic memory. The brain stores and processes it automatically without any conscious effort. The process of this information is called pre-attentive processing, which means the processing happens before paying attention to the information.

Procedural memory:

These are called motor skills. The prefrontal cortex, parietal cortex, and cerebellum are engaged in learning motor skills. Especially cerebellum is essential to coordinate the flow of movements required to learn a new skill, and also the timing of movements.

According to psychologists, procedural memory is nothing but a person's character. The theory is based on learning certain behaviors or emotional causes them to give automatic responses to specific situations. This reinforces good habits but also makes it difficult to leave bad habits. Damage to the cerebellum and basal ganglia affect procedural learning.

Explicit memory or declarative memory:

This memory is used to remember the appointment timing or recalling an event from the past. Remembering a song learned in childhood is an example of explicit memory. It can be divided into two categories, like episodic memory and semantic memory.

The **Episodic memory** contains visual information of a particular life event. It allows the mental time travel to recall various contexts and situational details of previous experiences.

Semantic memory relates to concepts and facts. An example of semantic memory includes types of food, the lexicon of a language or capital cities.

Stress is a major factor that affects explicit or declarative memory. You might be surprised to know that sleep has a vital role to play in your explicit or declarative memory. Sleep plays an active role in the strengthening and the amalgamation of your declarative memory. The unique property of sleep is that it helps in the reactivation of newly learned memories greatly enhances memory consolidation.

Implicit memory or non-declarative memory:

The implicit memory allows humans to do things by routine. It is not easy to verbalize it as the actions are performed without any effort. Implicit memory is like priming. The human brain is primed by their experiences, or something heard repeatedly, you are forced to recall the one which you heard frequently. For example, if someone asks you to name an American city which starts with the letter "N," many people would answer New York, unless you have exposure to Nampa, Naples, Nashville, etc.

Both implicit and explicit memory represents different ways of remembering the information.

Strategy to Strengthen Your Memory Pathway:

1. Identify Neural patterns that work in unique ways.
2. Promote the strength of desired memory-related neural circuitry.
3. Develop the ability to repeat the same pattern of sending information to evoke the same memory
4. Learning to utilize memory for guiding your behavior, performing, and acquiring new information, etc.

Astounding Psychological Facts about Brain

Brain Fact 1: Your reading speed increases when you use sans-serif fonts instead of serif fonts.

Reason: The Serif has a tiny extra-appendage feature, which increases the information processing demand. This increases the cognitive load. The brain has slightly more information to process and spends more time in comprehending the visual features and consciously deciphering its content.

Brain Fact 2: In right-handed people, moving eyes from left to right for 30 seconds temporarily improves memory for recently learned content.

Reason: While moving your eyes from side to side, you are actively engaging both hemispheres of the brain. This cross-lateral connection or cross-talk is very beneficial.

Brain Fact 3: Desserts served on round plates are perceived as sweeter than sharp-edged plates

Reason: Cross-modal perception is integrated into our perception. S, round plates are abstracted with sweetness, and sharp-edged plates are perceived as saltier or less-sweet.

Brain Fact 4: Coffee is expected to be more aromatic when served in narrow mugs.

Reason: This is caused by cross-modal perception. We assumed that the aroma is likely to be 'concentrated' due to the narrower opening of a glass.

Brain Fact 5: All Neurons undergo a recruitment process. Some neurons win. The brain recruits the best neurons. These recruited neurons stay and represent information and leave the rest, which is destroyed.

Reason:

1. Some neurons are better suited for representing

specific memory and learning.

2. Natural variation in neurons like cell structure, their location, etc. may deem some neurons superior and some inferior.

Brain Fact 6: Fake It Till You Make It

This works! You can fake anything you desire until you make it. Fake a smile to become happier. After systematically analyzing over 138 studies, researchers found strong evidence to show that smiling can surely make you happy. In the same way, you can fake confidence until you feel confident.

Reason: This is a scientific method. Follow The Scientific Method To overcome The "I Can't Do This" Inner Voice

Step 1: Assume that you do not know if you can do it

Step 2: Clearly define what you want to do

Step 3: Adopt a strategy to do it

Step 4: Start execution

Step 5: Periodically reflect on what has happened and repeat the steps frequently to improve the outcome.

TRY IT!

Brain Fact 7: Very similar sensory mechanisms perceive our pain and heat. It is tough to differentiate between the two.

Reason: The same sensory receptors called 'TRPV1' on the skin send a signal for both pain and heat. The sensory receptors neutrally send the same message through the same pathway. For us, our perception of pain and heat is different based on our knowledge and experience of what caused the pain, the emotional burden of that pain, our expectations, and our reactions to it. Our regular and frequent reactions further fuel our feelings and intensify them manifold, through recurring positive feedback loops.

Brain Fact 8: Multitasking is possible provided one of the tasks is highly automatic, and you are well versed and expert at switching quickly between the two tasks. It is task -switching. Anyone, with constant practice, can gain the necessary expertise and perform two or more complex tasks simultaneously through practice. For example, playing two guitars at a time.

Reason: Our brain focuses attention only on one single area at a time because focus and concentration demand a lot of neural resources. Biologically speaking, it is not economical to focus on multiple things simultaneously. However, this is not a complete picture. The fact is that humans can 'automate' activities where the attentional demands are quite low. So, by quick shifts in the attention, you can allow your body to act with ease and flawlessly. However, you must rehearse the activity and gain mastery over it. Often, we watch singers in the musical band play the guitar while singing and piano players synchronize both hands independently and eloquently.

Brain Fact 9: People like faces that match their name more than faces that don't match their name. This is called Cross-modal congruence. When people feel information from one sense matches with information from a different sense, they are happy. This, more often than not, is the basis of naming babies and pets. The research also shows that during elections, people tend to cast vote in favor of the candidate whose name matches his or her face.

Reason: Take, for instance, Arnold Schwarzenegger, the heavily built brawny man. Just imagine him named 'Tom.' It does not sound right to me. I know it does not sound right to you too. Well, this is because there is a tendency for the brain to prefer cross-modal congruence, that is, a preferred liking for sensory features that match each other. This is the reason why designers feel and insist a product shape is a lion and not a rat. It is for the same reason why artists think a specific color does not depict a context or situation correctly. We experience a particular satisfaction and contentment when there is 'congruence' between 2 sensory elements.

Brain Fact 10: For school and college students, it is more effective to study 2 or 3 similar topics in parallel in small chunks than many hours of study on a single topic.

Reason: This study method combines two processes called 'Interleaving' and 'chunking.' There is ample evidence to prove its efficacy. The simple logic here is that two or three similar topics are loaded with information that fits automatically into the broader framework. If you want to score well, you must practice Interleaving as it helps you learn similar concepts simultaneously. Activation of this neural & cognitive framework for related topics helps to:

1. Strengthen the overall framework

2. Strengthen the several components of the framework

3. Prevents over learning

4. Digesting information as parts or chunks. This allows better encoding of information that is grouped conceptually.

5 Lessons Your Brain Teaches You:

5 aspects of the brain that teach us valuable lessons to help us live a good, purposeful, and meaningful life!

Lesson 1: **Astrocytes**: The brain teaches you to appreciate the silent helpers that work for your benefit.

Lesson 2: Neural plasticity Learn and adapt. It is not too late

Lesson 3: Inhibition and excitation: Find an 'on' switch that is useful to you.

Lesson 4: Synaptic pruning: Do away with dead weight and try to optimize the available resources.

Lesson 5: Risk intuition of the adolescent brain:

Accept that some risks are beyond your control and comprehension. Be wise enough to take preventive measures.

Accept that some risks are beyond your comprehension and take preventive measures even if you do not fully understand the risks.

Chapter 4: A Comparison Between A Computer and Human Brain

Usually, many of us compare the human brain to a computer.

For an overview, you might think that computers and humans are not very different because both humans and computers have the same basic functions —input, storage, processing, and output.

But how correct is this? Before arriving at a conclusion, firstly, let us check the similarities and differences between the two.

Similarities in their functionality:

1. Our brain is a central processor of information while a computer has a central processing unit
2. Our brain takes sensory input → processes it/makes sense → produces behavior as output. Computers work similarly: information input →

processes the input → produces output.

3. Our body is essentially hardware, and the software comprises what we learn from informal life experiences and formal education. Computers require both hardware and software to function.

4. Our body as a system is a group of interdependent biochemical processes and signaling systems between different cells and organs. Computers work similarly (databases, services, and front end-user interface that interact with each other to carry out functions).

Component-wise similarities between a computer and human brain:

1. The graphics card in computers is similar to the visual cortex where virtual information is processed by the brain.

2. The sound card might be seen as the auditory cortex, where we process auditory information in the brain.

3. The hard drive, where memory is stored, might be the hippocampus. It is a crucial memory area. It is in the temporal lobe.

4. The processor or CPU could be the prefrontal cortex, which is associated with planning, thinking, and

problem-solving. RAM can also be put into the prefrontal cortex as it could be seen as similar to our short-term or working memory.

5. We might see the sensory cortex as a mouse or a keyboard, which collect input information from the outside world.

6. And finally, the motor cortex, which coordinates our movements, might be seen as similar to speakers or a monitor, how a computer outputs to the world.

If humans and computers do work similarly, then we might expect similar abilities. However, this is not always true. For example, let us ask two questions from a six-year-old child and a computer. As the first question, give a big calculation to both of them. The child will not be able to do it, whereas the computer can. As the second question, write a two-digit number on a board, say '67' in CAPTCHA style. When asked, the child immediately answers, whereas the computer does not. These types of puzzles, called CAPTCHAS, have been specifically designed to stop computers.

So, how do we account for this dramatic difference in what humans and computers can do? It turns out that brains and computers are very different, in terms of how they function, with memory being an excellent example of this.

Computers work by collecting and storing information in units, similar to how you would store books on a bookshelf. When they want to access data, they search through millions of files in these units to find it. They either have the information, or they do not. Brains, on the other hand, store memories in a very different way. Rather than each memory being held in a single storage container, they are characterized by a network of neural activations across the brain. An apple, for example, might activate "red," 'fruit,' a particular smell and a taste sensation. The more times the memory is activated, more firm, this specific pattern of activation becomes, and the stronger the memory. With billions of neurons and endless combinations of activation possible, the storage possibilities are tremendous.

We also know that thinking of the brain in terms of specific regions like computer components is not very accurate. In reality, the brain is one organ, and its functions are not divided into regions neatly. The hippocampus, for example, is not the only part of the brain responsible for memory and most other areas do several different jobs too. So, why can't computers work out the CAPTCHA number? Well, the computer hasn't seen the number written in this particular way before, so it can't fit it into one of its neat boxes. The child, on the other hand, does not depend on a single representation of the number written. So, when he sees the number, it activated memories in all different contexts, fonts, and colors. He may never have seen the number in this precise way before, but there is enough activation in the brain to tell him that it said '67' nonetheless. Humans are very good at generalizing, and they can get the gist of something even when they are looking at something new. This is not something that computers have been very good at, well at least, until now. Because the human brain is so successful, computer scientists have tried to copy the way it works. Artificial neural networks, inspired by those found in the brain, have been used to improve the performance of computers in areas such as image recognition, precisely the area CAPTCHAs exploit to stop computers now. By copying how the brain works, fooling computers might not be so easy in the future.

Advantages of the human brain over a computer:

- The human brain can invent computers, whereas computers cannot.

- Human brains feel emotions, fall in and out of love, enjoy music and a good joke, worry about the future, taste the flavor of a banana, and are self-aware, whereas, computers do not as they follow only the given coded instructions.

- Humans can be flexible in making decisions based on the situation, but Computers cannot.

- The human brain does not need any power to run, whereas a computer needs power to run. A supercomputer needs about 10,000 watts to run.

- Human brain costs nothing to create, whereas a lot of money is required to create a computer. A supercomputer costs tens of millions of dollars to create.

- The annual operating cost of the human brain is nothing, while that of a computer is very high.

- The size of the human brain is small, whereas that of a computer is very large.

Disadvantages of the human brain over a computer:

- Computers work at high speed while a human brain cannot. While a powerful computer can process about 8.2 billion megaflops, the human brain can process only about 2.2 megaflops.

- Computers give very accurate results, while humans may not always be very accurate.

- Computers do not suffer from boredom and tiredness and can work diligently, whereas humans cannot.

- Humans are not as versatile as computers.

- Once any data are stored in a computer, it can be retrieved at any point of time. This does not happen with humans.

- Computers are used by physically challenged people (for example, Stephen Hawking) to speak, and in other ways too, but humans cannot assist similarly.

Which is better - Computer or Human brain?

Many of you would say that the computer is better. But many scientists have been trying to make a computer as smart as a human brain. But when we compare the processor of a computer to the human brain, it cannot be compared, as the human brain is an organ and processor in a computer is an electronic component. Though there are similarities between the two, there are many differences too.

A computer has a set of instructions (program) that tells it what to do in addition to a memory that contains all the data and processor that goes and gets the instruction and applies them to the data one at a time in a sequence in a very orderly manner. On the other hand, a brain does not have a program, separate processes, and memory.

The brain is made up of cells called neurons (the basic unit of the brain) which are, approximately, about more than 100 billion in number. A neuron is a small component which has input notes that transmit the information as output notes. Thus, neurons are a complete, complex network of cells (Neural network) in your brain. One can think of this as an electronic circuit inside a brain, but much more complex than any circuit in a robot or any supercomputer. Each neuron in the brain can take in thousands of inputs at a time and simultaneously, independently process them, and give out the answers. Also, it modifies its functioning randomly, and all this happens in its hundred billion or so neurons whereas a computer processor has many interconnected transistors, which may also be about 5 to 10 billion in numbers in high-end computers. But the complexity of the brain cannot be found in the computer processor as the design is very simple with serial connections connecting one transistor to another.

What you will find there are just the binary digits 0's and 1's, but in a human brain, you have different emotions which are not available in a computer. When you compare a human brain with a computer, definitely a computer is faster in processing and giving instantaneous results, how much ever complex the calculation may be. But the understanding which is in a human brain is not present in a computer. For example, if you happen to see a building at night, you will be able to identify the building even on the next day. Whatever you understand or learn every day, you gain experience out of it, and gradually, there is so much accumulation of information that very coolly and confidently, you will be able to do any task if those tasks are related to one another. A computer is not that brainy. It does not have a brain at all. It can do only what we tell it to do. But sometimes, we wish that the computer is also like our brain, and behave as human beings do. So, scientists are trying to create Neural networks in computers too, so that computers can also start doing most of the tasks human beings do. Though manufacturing it is not possible at all because of its complexity, scientists have opted for software simulations. With the help of this software, we make the computer understand and learn like human beings. It has a network with input and output nodes and in between, there are some hidden nodes where all the nodes connected and form a network. Whatever input you give to the input nodes of your computer, they are transmitted slowly forward, and you get an output. For instance, if somebody asks you if it is sunny, you will go out and look for certain necessary conditions that make a sunny day, like looking at the Sun, check if the sky is clear, and if there is sunlight, etc. Finally, after analyzing everything, you give a response that it is sunny.

In the same way, the artificial neural networks of a computer analyze the input; gradually, they proceed step by step where the answers for the keyed-in data may be 'yes' for a few and 'no' for a few other questions, and finally, we get an output, for us to understand. But we need a feedback network. For example, consider a case wherein you are playing basketball, and you need to throw the ball in the basket. Initially, you observe that when you try to throw the ball in the basket, it goes high, but falls very close to you and not in the basket. So, the next time you analyze that you have to exert some more force; it should not go very high and fall right into the basket. Gradually, by trying to throw the 5-6 times and by reducing the errors, you finally succeed to throw the ball in the basket.

In the same way, even in the neural network of computers, Backpropagation is added to improve the system, so that it does not make any repeated mistakes. Neural networks these days are used in Voice recognition, Handwriting recognition, or when you try to retrieve photos with the help of key text. In this way, neural networks are working to improve our lives, and these are copied from the human brain.

In the final analysis, the human brain is so powerful that the way it can think, analyze, and understand is not possible by a computer. For example, if you teach your computer to recognize a chair and show it a few chair samples, it can recognize only those and not a chair which is designed differently while a human brain very well can. Man has invented the computer, and it is difficult to compare brain and computer because they work in completely different ways.

That is why if anyone asks you, which is smarter or intelligent- a Computer or Human brain, of course, you know the answer.

Chapter 5: Brain Health

Solving The Puzzle: Everything You Need To Know About Your Brain and Brain Health

Knowledge about the Mysteries of the mind gives you the cutting-edge which surpasses and transcends all information you have gathered over the years. This knowledge is power in the palm of your hand.

"When you become the master of your mind,

You become a master of everything."

- Swami Satchidananda

Know Your Brain- The True You

- Your brain determines every aspect of your life, and without your brain, there is no self and no awareness of the world.

- Your brain is a three-pound universe.

- Your brain is powerful.

- The electricity generated by your brain can power a

bulb.

- Your brain is a non-stop worker. It works for 24 hours a day and 7 days a week.

- Your brain is made of 100 billion neurons, 500 trillion synapses traveling at 300 miles/hour speed.

- Your brain is always busy. When you think, see, or move, electrical signals race among billions of neurons.

- Your brain is resilient. Its neuroplasticity allows it to adapt and respond to change.

- Your brain is amazing. It creates thoughts, drives, emotions, and stores memories.

- Your brain gets better with use.

Why Brain Health matters:

As the world population ages, there will be more and more dementia cases. Dementia means the brain loses its abilities, such as memory and communication skills. It can be caused by strokes, narrowed or clogged arteries, blocking blood flow, and head injuries.

Injuries to the Left Side of the Brain causes:

- Difficulty in understanding languages.

- Difficulties in speaking languages.

- Depression and anxiety.

- Verbal memory deficiency.

- Impaired logical thinking.

- Sequential difficulties.

- Decreasing control over body movements on the right side.

Injuries to the Right Side of the Brain causes:

- Visual and spatial impairment.

- Visual memory deficiency.

- Decreased awareness of body deficiencies.

- Loss of comprehensive, or "the big picture" type of thinking.

- Decreasing control over body movements on the left side.

The Haunting Memory Loss Problem:

Memory loss disrupts your daily life. Dementia is a general term for a decline in mental ability, and Alzheimer's is the most common brain disease that causes a slow decline in memory, thinking, and reasoning skills. There are warning signs and symptoms. When you notice any one of them, please do not ignore them.

Alarming Health Statistics:

- In 2003, approximately 27.7 million people worldwide were diagnosed with dementia.

- The number grew to 46.8 million in 2015.

- It is expected to reach 75 million in 2030 and 131 million in 2050.

Disturbing findings:

- Approximately 5 million Americans today are living with Alzheimer's.

- One hundred thirty-five million Americans are expected to be affected by 2050.

- Forty-five million people globally are dementia patients.

  Take action today.

11 Early Signs and Symptoms of Memory loss:

Memory loss disrupts daily life in many ways:

1. Mood shifts and personality disorders
2. Budget management very difficult
3. Poor decision-making skills
4. Difficulty having a conversation
5. Problem solving and planning become a challenge
6. Difficulty in doing routine household chores
7. Unable to speak or write words
8. Losing things and unable to trace them
9. Withdrawal from work or social activities

Take action now to improve your Brain Health. Do not procrastinate.

The power to remember IS IN YOUR HANDS

6 Pillars of Brain Health

Your brain health is profoundly dependent on what you

drink and eat, your exercise routine, how soundly you sleep, the way, and how frequently you socialize, and the way you manage stress.

1. Food and Nutrition

What you eat affects your productivity in different ways, so eat smart.

. The fact is that different foods affect your work performance. A recent study of dietary habits revealed exciting results. Participants reported their food consumption, mood, and behaviors over 13 days. The study showed that the participants who ate more fruits and vegetables and less high-fat meals were happier, more creative, and more productive than those who ate high-fat, and high-calorie meals.

Opt for a Mediterranean diet. This diet is found to be rich in whole grains, fish, green leafy vegetables, nuts, and olives. This diet improves brain health. It reduces the risk of Alzheimer's disease. **2. Physical Exercise**

Exercise adds life to your years. It helps you lose weight, keeps your bones and your brain healthy, boosts your mood, improves your sleep, reduces your risk of cancer and heart disease. A regular exercise regime reduces your risk of lifestyle-oriented diseases like heart disease, diabetes, obesity, and some kinds of cancers. By exercising regularly, you can keep dementia and Alzheimer's disease at bay. Exercise improves blood flow in the body and your memory. It stimulates specific chemical changes in the brain, which enhances thinking, learning, and mood. Always be fit and smart.

3. Living in tune with Nature

It is an excellent stress reliever. While some amount of stress is essential as it motivates you to meet the challenges of life, *excess* stress causes your body to produce the stress hormone Cortisol which is strongly linked to health problems, such as depression, dementia, insomnia, heart disease, and many more.

Hiking in a natural area or strolling briefly outside, having green plants in your office or looking out the window at the trees is found to be effective ways to cause a measurable drop in Cortisol. Research results show that participants who took a 30-minute walk regularly lowered their cortisol levels significantly.The World Health Organization recommends 150 minutes of exercise per week for adults.

4. Sleep and Relaxation

Without a good night's sleep, you are not going to remember the next day. That 6-8 hour window is one of the crucial windows of sleep. It is REM sleep, and if you do not get that, you are not going to remember what you learned during the day, and you are not going to be prepared for the next day in terms of your memory.

Naps refresh and rejuvenate you. A short nap in the afternoon increases your cognitive function for the rest of the day. You must take a nap when you feel drowsy, and when your energy levels are low.

- **Planned Nap**. Including a nap sometime after midday will help you stay alert to accommodate a late-night study or a weekend celebration
- **Emergency Nap**: It is a sign of prolonged sleep-deprivation. If you feel you need to take a nap before a crucial activity, it indicates that you are not getting sufficient night's sleep.
- **Habitual Nap**: It is a habit among kids and adults, and is very beneficial.

5. Medical Health

Several health issues like obesity, diabetes, high blood pressure disrupt brain functioning. Keeping your blood pressure and weight at an optimum and healthy level, taking medication as prescribed, cutting down on sugar and salt, staying active, positive and socially connected helps you stay smart, sharp, and increase your vitality and quality of life.

- **Drink plenty of water**

  A dehydrated brain is a brain that won't be able to focus. So, that is why drinking plenty of water is essential.

- **Obesity**

  Many studies affirm the fact that overweight people are more likely to develop diabetes, and diabetic patients have a much higher risk of getting dementia.

- **Weight management:**
  - Avoid white flour, white sugar, and hydrogenated fat.
  - Eat more and more fiber.
  - Eat sufficient protein with every meal.
  - Control your portion size.

- Exercise for at least 20-30 minutes 5 times a week.
- Do Yoga, Pranayama and meditation

- **Hypertension**

  High blood pressure can cause irreparable structural damage in the brain. It causes a gradual mental decline.
  - Cut down on salt.
  - Regular blood pressure check-up.
  - Avoid a sedentary lifestyle.
  - Maintain a proper, healthy weight.
  - Take all your medicines on time and regularly.

6. Mental Fitness

- **Fight Depression**

  Depression is a health issue that is afflicting the world population. Nearly 17 million Americans are affected by it every year. We must understand that depression is not a normal part of growing older.

Train Yourself to Be Happier. Your happiness is within you. Do not search for happiness outside.

- **Stay Positive**

  Ups and downs are a part of life. Develop Resilience. You must consciously increase your ability to bounce back from difficult situations. Learning to be more resilient can help you stay healthy and positive in the face of daily upsets, as well as significant life events. Staying positive enhances your resilience, boosts self-esteem, helps you adapt to change, and encourages you to take risks, and even accept failure as part of your life.

Manage Stress

Stress symptoms:

'STRESS' is unavoidable in your life that will express itself as:

1. Not able to sleep at night.
2. Sudden angry outbursts, frustration, and depression that affect your relationships and family life.
3. Emotional disturbance and inability to concentrate.

4. Anxiety about the outcome, or constant worry, or fear.

5. Depression or fear of failure.

6. Physical symptoms, such as headaches, stomach aches, ulcers, nausea.

7. Trying to avoid going to work.

Be cheerful. The good news is Stress is manageable. Maria Jahoda (1963) proposed the following six characteristics of the mentally healthy individual:

1. Environmental Mastery
2. Undistorted perception of reality
3. Integration
4. Autonomy
5. Growth, self-development, and self-actualization
6. Attitude towards Self

Health Perspectives:

1. Sense of Responsibility.
2. Sense of self-reliance.
3. Sense of Direction.
4. A set of personal values.
5. Sense of individuality.
6. Mental well-being.
7. Lack of mental disorder.
8. Cultural and religious considerations.

Social Life and Relationships

Stay connected with peers, friends, and family members through a vibrant social network are the best sources of support. It reduces stress and anxiety, combats depression, and enhances your intellectual stimulation. Studies have shown that regular social interaction slows down the rate of memory decline. Happy marriages, healthy family life, and stable long term relationships provide significant protection against age-related cognitive impairment.

So, make new friendships. Treasure your loved ones, and cherish your childhood friends.

Planned vacation:

Relax during your weekends. Working through the weekend is both unproductive and unhealthy. You must take time off work as it is healthy for your body, mind, and relationships. The average American takes only half of this earned vacation leave. The people you meet and the time you spend must add value to your life.

10 Ways To Disconnect From Work:

1. Switch off during the weekend.

2. Find a place you can escape to.

3. Keep a to-do list.

4. Make your weekend fun.

5. Focus on the art of being L'art de Vivre.

6. Delegate while at work.

7. Find a hobby.

8. Keep a separate work zone at home.

9. Turn your notifications off. Switching off your smartphone alerts can reduce stress.

10. Manage time properly.

Why you need to disconnect at the weekend:

1. Taking time off makes you more productive. A Report from the Business Round Table showed that Working 60-hours per week for two months cause a decrease in productivity equivalent to having just worked 40-hours per week in the first place.

2. Your mind has work to do even when it is not working: The human brain has essential processing to do during 'wakeful rest,' which may improve memory and problem-solving.

3. Resting properly can help you love your job. Researchers compelled a group of workaholics to

take a regular break. The employees reported greater job satisfaction, and work and life balance and were more likely to stay with their company long-term.

4. Your performance ratings will improve. The results of an internal study by Ernst & Young found that every additional 10-hours of vacation improved employees' year-end performance rating, by nearly 8%.

5. Sitting too much can be fatal. A 12 years study by 'The Women's Health Initiative ' indicated a reduced lifespan for women who spent long periods sitting down.

6. A vacation is a temporary solution. We need to rest, but studies have shown that the benefits of a vacation can fade within 2-4 weeks- suggesting the need for a regular weekend top-up.

7. Overtime can make you depressed. Regardless of chronic physical disease, smoking, alcohol use, job strain, and work-related social support, long-hours can double the chances of a major depressive episode.

8. A change of scene makes you more creative.

Spending time in a different culture can improve associative and idea-generating skills.

9. Relaxing is good for your health and professional life.

10. Extra work days mean extra stress.

11. Heavy computer use leads to eye strain and worse. A Japanese study has found a connection between the temporary eye strain that computer work can cause, and the development of glaucoma, which can lead to blindness.

12. Working long hours causes cardiovascular problems. A study of 195 men aged 30-69 showed that working 11 hours or more could double the chance of a heart attack.

13. Stress from work alienates your relationships. A psychological study showed that spouses who were stressed from work were less and more anxious in their relationships.

Brain Health Assessment:

Your brain health includes Thinking processes, Emotional processes, Biological processes, and Learned behaviors.

QUIZ   What Is Your Brain Type: Questions To Discover Your Brain Type

These questions are on your physical or biological, mental, emotional, learned behavior, etc.

1. Your organization is excellent

   Never-   Very   Rarely-   Only   Occasionally – Frequently- Very Frequently

2. Get distracted easily

   Never-   Very   Rarely-   Only   Occasionally – Frequently- Very Frequently

3. Attention span is poor

   Never-   Very   Rarely-   Only   Occasionally – Frequently- Very Frequently

4. It is easy to be patient and wait inline

   Never-   Very   Rarely-   Only   Occasionally – Frequently- Very Frequently

5. Lose train of thought in the middle of talking about something.

   Never-   Very   Rarely-   Only   Occasionally – Frequently- Very Frequently

6. Have trouble delaying gratification

Never- Very Rarely- Only Occasionally – Frequently- Very Frequently

7. Struggle with memory

Never- Very Rarely- Only Occasionally – Frequently- Very Frequently

8. Memory is worse than it was ten years ago

Never- Very Rarely- Only Occasionally – Frequently- Very Frequently

9. Having trouble remembering names

Never- Very Rarely- Only Occasionally – Frequently- Very Frequently

10. Exercise more than twice per week.

Never- Very Rarely- Only Occasionally – Frequently- Very Frequently

11. Get at least 7-8 hours of sleep a day

Never- Very Rarely- Only Occasionally – Frequently- Very Frequently

12. The Diet tends to be poor and haphazard

Never- Very Rarely- Only Occasionally – Frequently- Very Frequently

13. Drink more than two normal sizes (8 ounces) cups of coffee a day.

Never- Very Rarely- Only Occasionally – Frequently- Very Frequently

14. Drink sugar-sweetened soda every day.

    Never- Very Rarely- Only Occasionally – Frequently- Very Frequently

15. Have more than four average size alcoholic drinks each week

    Never- Very Rarely- Only Occasionally – Frequently- Very Frequently

16. Smoke cigarettes or cigars or exposed to secondhand smoke

    Never- Very Rarely- Only Occasionally – Frequently- Very Frequently

17. Spend more than an hour a day watching TV.

    Never- Very Rarely- Only Occasionally – Frequently- Very Frequently

18. Having trouble getting and staying asleep

    Never- Very Rarely- Only Occasionally – Frequently- Very Frequently

19. Under high stress at home or home

    Never- Very Rarely- Only Occasionally – Frequently- Very Frequently

20. Involved in new learning activities or brain training games

    Never- Very Rarely- Only Occasionally – Frequently- Very Frequently

21. How have you been feeling lately:
    a. Tend to notice what is wrong more than what is right.

    b. Tend to be argumentative or oppositional.

    c. Thoughts tend to loop and get stuck in mind.

    d. Struggle with feeling sad or blue.

    e. Struggle with worry.

    f. Having trouble letting go of hurts from the past.

    g. Thoughts are negative.

    h. Self-esteem is perfect.

    i. Having trouble experiencing joy.

    j. Tend to take things the wrong way.

    k. Have difficulty relaxing.

    l. Bite fingernails or pick at the skin.

    m. Feel nervous and tense.

    n. Energy level most days is excellent.

Chapter 6: Harnessing Your Brain Power

We hypnotize ourselves with our words or thoughts. While starting any work if you start thinking that you are a big failure, you will fail in that work. Vice-versa also very true, i.e., if you start a work thinking that you can do it successfully, then definitely the result will be a success only. So, our thoughts impact our self-image.

When fate closes all doors, it is faith in the BRAIN POWER that opens new doors.

Match your brain span with your life span:

You are your brain. Your brain determines the physical, mental, emotional, spiritual, and every aspect of your life.

Develop A Good Memory:

Storing information in the brain is more or less an automatic process of holding on to information in the brain. It can be stored in short-term memory, sensory memory, or long-term memory. Each stage of these different human memory act as a filter to protect you from the vast flood of information that challenges you every moment of the day. The more the information is used or repeated, the more it will be retained in long-term memory; that is why a repeated study helps people to perform better in exams.

Build Your Brain Reserve

The reserve that helps your brain to understand and respond, make decisions, adapt to changes, and resist damage is known as 'Brain reserve.' You develop your brain reserve from childhood, and the brain reserve gets stronger as you move through your youth and adulthood. You can build and improve your brain reserve when you continue to learn, develop new skills, and embrace new activities and interests.

Increase Your Intelligence Quotient:

Your subconscious mind is a potent tool. When properly harnessed, your brain gives you the ability to become whatever you want in life effortlessly. Your subconscious mind works like an enormous impression or memory bank. It has unlimited capacity and stores permanently each and everything that you come across in your life.

Your subconscious mind, mainly stores and retrieves information. It also ensures that the response will be precise as you are programmed. Your subconscious mind does everything you say and match with your self-concept. You can program your subconscious mind by repeating positive affirmations.

Let's imagine that the conscious mind is the gardener who plants the seeds, and the subconscious mind is like fertile that help the seed to germinate and grow in the soil. So, by harnessing the brain, it is possible to modify your entire thought process. Thoughts create associations or links, they form layer upon layer, and then they will become thick and deeper.

If you can visualize your brain as a library, the page which you are reading currently is your consciousness. The pages which you are completing reading are your subconscious mind, the big storage area. The human brain does not forget anything. Every detail, right from your first day at school is still printed in mind somewhere down to what you ate for breakfast or what color of a dress your partner is wearing. All this information is not ordinarily available to access. However, just like the library stack, you need a unique process to access the information. Usually, the conscious mind does the filtration of information that is not required.

Key Benefits Of Harnessing The Brain:

- Enhanced relationships.
- Improved health and wellbeing.
- Higher levels of creativity.
- Problem-solving capabilities.
- More relaxed and composed.
- The ability to transcend limiting beliefs.
- Creating a feeling of happiness and purpose in your life.
- Sense of control and empowerment.

Limitless opportunities will come your way. Take the first and right step to boost your chances of success and achieve it NOW. Psychological tactics when judiciously used will make a massive difference to your LIFE. You could achieve your dreams, the burning desires you cherished in your heart for years, and move slowly and steadily towards Total Self Actualization.

Success is 1% inspiration and 99% perspiration in the right direction with perseverance, will-power, and commitment.

How To Develop Brain Power

We all know that if you have a sharp memory, you will have knowledge. If you have knowledge, then there is no dearth of success in life. A powerful memory can change the entire course of your life, but most of us face the problem of forgetting things. You want to recall something, but you cannot retrieve it. There are also instances where you have a set point, and you are unable to reach it, and you feel like a failure.

But that is the wrong conditioning in your brain. You must flip that around and turn a problem into a project, or a problem into a challenge.

Everyone wants answers to questions like how to flip wrong conditioning in your brain, or how to boost your brainpower, or how to keep your mind sharp?

The good news is that regular daily activities of a particular type can provide a solution to the above questions, and also help us have a robust memory deep into our 70s and 80s too.

"Watchword: Be quick, but not in a hurry." —Coach John Wooden

It's a matter of control. Happy are the ones who are busy pursuing realistic goals. They do not give up until they reach their target. People who have attainable goals reaped several physical and psychological benefits, including:

- Absence of negative affect and depression symptoms.
- Lower levels of cortisol.
- Lesser systemic inflammation.
- Optimum immune functioning.
- Fewer mental and physical health problems in the long-run.

Adopt these powerful and proven techniques for **Clearing, Energizing,** and **Balancing** your brain if you want to improve your memory.

Strategies For Better Memory

You meet someone. You can even remember where you met

the person. But his name? It is just out of reach, eludes you, taunting you.

You think and accept it as part of growing older and feel helpless about it. However, it is this attitude that makes things even worse. The good news is, by focusing on your inherent potential and continuing to exercise your mind, you may boost your memory power. Get started with these tips to keep your brain as sharp as a fiddle.

Listed below are a few of such daily activities to be followed:

1. **Approach Life Differently**
   - Have a plan
   - Keep things simple
   - Create and pursue focused goals
   - Focus on making small continuous improvements
   - Focus on productivity, and not on being busy
   - Make logical and informed decisions
   - Constantly learn
   - Be willing to fail
   - Learn from mistakes
   - Measure and track your progress
   - Spend time with motivated people

- Maintain a positive attitude.
- Rest and recharge
- Set realistic boundaries
- Maintain balance in life

2. **Take On New Challenges**

Keep challenging your brain daily: Learning a new skill, or doing activities that get you thinking are great for your brain health and helps to maintain its function longer. The well-known adage, 'If you do not use it, you will lose it' is very true. So, the more active you keep your brain, the healthier it will be, and the longer it will work well for you. The more you practice, speaking, thinking, problem-solving, the better you will be able to do it, and the longer you will be able to do it well.

So, take classes, learn a foreign language, do brain teasers, talk about controversial or complex topics, read a book, and discuss what you read. These things will help you lay down new memories and strengthen the connections in the brain pathways that are very important for healthy brain function. The denser and stronger these pathways are, the better you will be able to remember.

Studies show that the human brain is very conducive to new learning. Researchers put adult mice in a highly stimulating environment. After a few days, they found that their cell communication and brain structure changed in ways. There was a visible improvement in the animals' ability to learn and recall newly-learned behaviors. The same is true in the human brain too. Repeatedly doing the same activity is not as helpful as taking on new learning activities. Always look forward to taking up fresh mental challenges. If you have excellent computer skills, challenge yourself to solve crossword puzzles, or learn a new language.

3. Control Life's Stressors

Anxiety is your brain's worst threat. Stressful experiences, such as grief, relocating, losing a job, financial problems, etc. adversely affect and limit your brain's ability to store and recall information. Studies show that when we are stressed up, hormones known as glucocorticoids are released, which, in excess, damaged brain cells. As stress cannot always be avoided, having some control over it is less of a burden to your body and mind. The worst enemy to your memory is stress. Think about a time in your life when you were stressed out, or you were going through a stressful period in your life. Your memory was probably horrible. So, to reduce your stress, some people meditate, or close their eyes and exhale and clear their mind and have a quiet time. Avoid stress whenever possible.

4. Be More Organized

You can declutter your mind by creating a Brain Dump. Organize all your life activities in your brain with a brain dump.

A brain dump is a repository to unload all the random, and diverse thoughts swirling about in your mind. This helps you focus on one concept and one idea at a time. The truth is that your tasks, your chores, your daily worries overwhelm you very often, and tend to distract you regularly from the tasks you need to do.

You can do it in a matter of minutes and requires a little planning. It gives you the necessary mental clarity to focus on your more important tasks. All your scattered thoughts are pooled, then organized and followed up with ease. It takes the mental load off-it is very relaxing.

It takes you just 10 minutes or even less. A regular brain dump done at the end of each day keeps you well-prepared for the next morning. You can thus, start your new day without worrying or overthinking about all the things you have to do. If a daily brain dump is not possible, you can stick to a weekly schedule.

Your Brain dump saves you a lot of time and effort. When you write down your thoughts, you are no longer weighed down by scattered thoughts which create a chaotic atmosphere in your brain. Your brain is decluttered of unnecessary information. It is now calm and ready to give optimum output. With practice, it becomes a habit. It saves you a lot of time, energy, and maximizes your productivity. Regular brain dumps are a sure way to reach your much-cherished goals in life.

5. **Develop Neuroplasticity**

Neuroplasticity is the brain's ability to think creatively, make new connections, and learn new behaviors. It encompasses all activities like learning a new language, playing an instrument, our attitudes, moods, ambitions, and outlook. Counseling, therapy, meditation, breath awareness, physical exercise are all examples of activities that can support neuroplasticity.

Exposing the brain to novel experiences is the ideal way to develop the brain's neuroplasticity. The brain, like a curious kid, responds dramatically to anything new. Brain scans reveal this functioning of the brain. A regular meditation practice, for example, enhances the brain's ability to regulate emotion as it causes an increased folding of the outer layer. Meditation also induces a shift in activity from the right to the left prefrontal cortex. It transforms your brain and resolves imbalances.

6. **Move Out Of The Comfort Zone Into The Growth Zone**

You can be in any one of the four Zones; if you genuinely love yourself, you will opt for the growth zone. In the Comfort Zone, you feel safe and in control. In the Fear Zone, you lack self-confidence and always find excuses to be affected by others' opinions. If you are in the Learning Zone, you deal with challenges and problems, acquire new skills and extend your Comfort Zone

However, when you enter the Growth Zone, you find your life purpose, live your dreams, set new goals, and conquer your objectives.

7. **Auto Suggestions And Hetero Suggestions**

Auto Suggestions: An auto-suggestion is a suggestion or self-talk you give to yourself. Your self-talk can either boost your ability to nourish your personal and professional life or ruin it.

Auto Suggestions, thus can be Positive Auto suggestions and Negative Auto suggestions.

Positive Auto suggestions: Self suggestions like I am happy. I am healthy; I am an excellent student. I am fun to be around, etc. boost our morale and self-esteem. Personal comments like I am feeling wonderful, and life is going great; this is another great day, etc. releases happiness hormones like dopamine, endorphins, and serotonin. Keep using them.

Negative Auto suggestions: These are the self-suggestions we must notice and watch out for. Self-talk like I cannot do that; I look ugly, I am tired and confused. It damages your sense of Self slowly and dangerously. You must root out from the mind and replace it with a positive one.

Hetero Suggestions: The suggestion that which is given by one or more persons to another, either verbally or mentally is a hetero suggestion. You can call it "let us put our heads together." or " two heads are better than one."

Positive Hetero Suggestions: Any statement you hear from others that makes you feel good about yourself and your ability is a Positive Hetero Suggestion. For example, comments like You look great today, Perfect Job, Such a tasty meal! etc will make you more cheerful and keep you rocking.

Negative Hetero Suggestions: These are remarks that hurt you and damage your self-esteem. Comments like You are inefficient. You work so slowly, your ideas never work. Such statements of criticism are not at all helpful. Keep them out of your mind. You must replace such negative statements from your mind with positive, supportive statements.

Nourish your mind with good mental food. Use Motivational cards like "I find happiness in all I do."

8. **Put An End To Overthinking:**

Thinking, this ability sets you apart from other animals. However, you must avoid overthinking, which is a very detrimental habit that causes chronic severe problems. Overthinking prevents you from living your optimum life. Overthinking fills you with doubt, pushes you into negative thinking, creates non-existent obstacles, clouds your judgment, and prevents you from taking decisive action, causes mental anguish, makes you anxious and depressed. It, thus, sucking all the joy and happiness from your life.

9. Practice Mindfulness

Be focused on the present moment. Mindfulness is about being aware of the present moment, focusing entirely on whatever is happening at the moment, and therefore, taking your thoughts away from the past or the future. Mindfulness is about taking in everything with all the five sense thinking about what is going on right now. If you are reading, don't just read mindlessly. Pay attention to every word you read while assimilating them. While eating, focus on the food, enjoy and feel the taste of the food you chew and eat. If you are bathing, focus falling on the water on your body. Feel its temperature. Listen to the sounds around you. Be prepared to take in the smells and sights around you. If you are working on something with your hands, take in its texture and how it feels in your hands. Enjoy the present moment.

10. **Maintain a balanced energy field**: Like the simple daily routine like brushing your teeth to prevent caries; you also need to clean your energy field using the Bio-field Daily Energy Balancing Exercise. It harmonizes and balances your nervous system, brain, and the functional energies of your chakra system and enhances your communication. You create your world by focusing on energy. Your intent drives the energy for whatever purpose needed.

Chapter 7: Improving Brain Health: A Multifaceted Approach

How Age Alters Memory

Aging can affect your memory in several ways. Memory problems are caused by hypothyroidism, stress, diabetes, depression, cardiovascular problems, and other illnesses. Alcohol, sleeping pills, and tranquilizers will affect the memory system.

Learn New Strategies To Improve Your Memory

You must improve your general memory, remembering capacity, and the skill of memorizing specific things. When our brain receives information from our senses, it gets some pre-memory raw information. In the brain, this information received from our senses leaves an impression or imprint only at the biological level. This imprint induces a minimal change in the communication of the neurons.

By adopting the following techniques, you can strengthen the neural circuitry, which plays a vital role in memory formation. Your recalling capacity of information will be better. You can improve brainpower.

1. **Visualization:**

Visualizing in a creative way is an act of painting a picture within your mind. It can influence your beliefs, and beliefs, in turn, shape the reality. It is a powerful tool to enact the Law of Attraction. Use strong and positive emotions, along with big, bright pictures when you are speaking to the unconscious mind. Also, use meditation to better access the subconscious mind and impact it faster.

2. Positive Affirmation:

Affirmations are the beliefs and values that you want to have in your life. Affirmations should be formed using meaningful words, which will evoke the feelings that you desire to feel after the manifestation of it. A gentle smile along with affirmation will bring forth a positive feeling instantly.

3. Sleep-Learning:

An excellent way to stimulate and harness the infinite power of your subconscious mind is sleep learning. It means you learn new things while you sleep. This technique enables you to learn foreign languages, pass your exams, undertake desired professional studies, and implement self-growth plans with great success. The recorded sound is used in this technique. Within 30 minutes of starting sleep, you need to play the sound. It is also known as Hypnopedia.

Within a short time, you will start thinking in a new way. With the aid of these new subconscious beliefs, you can take necessary action that helps you to achieve your cherished goals.

4. Meditation:

It is a potent tool and an effective method to access your subconscious mind. Meditation has vast benefits for both physical and psychological self. It helps to learn and unlock your subconscious mind. You can chant mantras or visualize an object while meditating. The goal of Meditation is to become more aware of your inner emotions and thoughts and changing the patterns of thoughts to create a higher awareness. With Meditation, all anxiety ends. At a deeper level, meditation is a doorway of getting to know yourself completely, both who you are inside, and how you react to what is outside.

Meditation transforms a wandering mind into a beautiful mind! Put aside at least 15-20 minutes in a day for meditation and yoga. Meditation, Yoga, and Pranayama result in a healthy and confident brain state.

Meditation is a great way to deprogram this anxious, instant gratification oriented brain. Meditation has a very long list of health benefits, many of which have been documented scientifically. There are far too many to talk about here, but one huge advantage is that it quiets that constantly talking usually negative inner narrator. The inner narrator is the one saying: I have to do this, I have to do that, what should I eat for lunch? How come so and so has not texted me back? And so on.

There is a network in the brain called the default mode network generating this mind chatter. It is responsible for thinking about yourself, thinking about how other people are thinking about you, and ruminating about the past, and worrying about the future.

Meditation has been shown to reduce activity in this network. For example, when someone is craving a cigarette, the posterior cingulate cortex strongly lights up. By reducing activity in the default mode network, meditation can help diffuse that anxious, impatient, unfocused, and instant gratification oriented mind that the internet helped to create.

5. Mantra Magic: Setting The Brain Free:

The Mantra is a powerful magnet which aligns your thoughts and attracts what you desire. Mantras weaken negative energies. Mantras generate positive energies. Chanting mantra changes our thoughts and lifestyle. Mantras aid to focus and calm the mind and bring clarity and peace.

How Mantra Works: **The Law Of Attraction** at work. While repeating a mantra, we echo certain words over and over again, that create specific energy vibrations. As like attracts like, these vibrations will then attract what you seek. Mantras manifest abundance and make all our dreams come true. Chant "OM Aham Aarogyam" I am healthy.

6. Linguistic Shift:

Third Person Positive Self-Talk deliberately creates some psychological distance. It helps to regulate your emotions. It reduces emotional overthinking, anxiety, and stress.

7. Spaced Repetition:

Simply repeating information in a structured manner after a short duration to strengthen it helps to improve the memory for it. For example, your list of medicines. You can repeat it aloud, or say mentally in your head. You can teach it to someone. You may repeat it to a family member, or your friend. In this technique, you repeat it after a while, then after a slightly longer duration, repeat after 5 minutes, then after 20, then in 2 hours, then in 6 hours, then in 12 hours, then the next day, then on alternate days, then after a week. In less than a week, you'll memorize it.

8. Deliberate Imagery:

This is a prevalent and beneficial memory-boosting technique. Your mind has the unlimited capability of conjuring and observing a lot of information. Visualizing an object or a firm intention creates a durable and lasting imprint in the brain. The more the number of details, the better it is to your memory and retention. Most of the information the brain receives has mental imagery. For example, to learn a chart or the process in a lecture, you can visualize it a few times, and rehearse it through your mind. Each time you do it, you improve the memory of it.

9. Snowballing Strategy:

Making associations between related bits of information immensely aid to improve memory formation. The brain enjoys and loves to create an association and network of information it receives. The stronger the related associations, the better will be the memory for all things that are associated. You can intentionally make strong associations between places you've visited, conversations, theories you've learned and the people you've met. You can also make associations by comparing two incidents and contrasting them, by linking them in several creative ways, by finding similarities, etc.

10. Practice and More Practice:

Memory champions, Musicians, writers, orators, etc. practice their trade and repeat it several times. They gain experience and a powerful memory by trying different but related things. Regular practice is very useful in developing unique and specialized circuitry in the brain. This helps you acquire 'new information' relevant to your profession.

11. Assign Additional Meaning:

You can develop your brainpower by making more and more associations, gathering more information, learning new things, memorizing new aspects, and expanding your knowledge about it. You'll thus form an extensive network. The greater the density of the network, the stronger will be the memory for all things on that particular network. Such networking builds neural circuitry across several regions of your brain. The more creative you are, the greater will be your memory.

12. Design Mind Maps:

A mind map is a sure memory enhancer. You can make a memory map in your head, or on paper to form stronger memories.

13. Attention Is The Surest Key to Form useful Memories:

The brain receives a lot of information all the time. The information the brain receives is either useful or useless. Consciously attend to useful information. This makes memory formation easier. Deliberately notice things and take mental notes for memory formation.

14. Giving Weight to Information:

You can selectively treat some information as more important and make it 'heavy' by assigning more weight to it. This works effectively to fine-tune and direct your brain to integrate and consolidate this 'heavy' information during the REM cycle of your sleep. The reason for this is that important, and 'heavy' information persuades and urges the brain to memorize it.

15. Mnemonics:

Mnemonics make information meaningful for the brain for restructuring it. Mnemonic requires organized and planned homework, and they are strategic mental tools. For example – How to give good response? F.A.S.T is the mnemonic for Forward, Actionable, Succinct, and Timely.

16. Stop Procrastinating:

Procrastination occurs when your brain thinks that the consequence of doing this task will be a painful experience. And thus, it intentionally tries to avoid it.

- Step 1: Identify the Cue

- Step 2: Change the Routine
- Step 3: Substitute Pain with Pleasure
- Step 4: Modify your existing belief patterns: Wipe away your "subconscious" limiting thoughts and beliefs in your subconscious mind.

You can avoid procrastination by dealing with it like it is a habit. Focus your willpower on The Cue, and create a plan to change your reaction to the task. You have the control to rewire your brain and thus, form new beneficial habits.

The process of dealing with procrastination:

1. Task assignment

2. Perceived pain

3. Aversion Activity

4. Intending to avoid procrastination

5. Identify the cue, the routine, and the reward

6. Change the Belief

7. Rebuild your habit

8. Practice

9. Say goodbye to procrastination

All the above practices may appear to be pretty simple and straightforward, but deviously hard to turn into a habit.

But, once they do become habits, they will generate far more motivation and willpower than they require.

Chapter 8: Changing Your Thinking Patterns

Tap the Power for Positive Change residing within your mind!

Correct The 4 Fundamental Flaws In Your Thinking Process:

Flaw 1 – A False dichotomy:

Thinking in black and white. Taking an extreme stance. Like it is good or bad, it is right for you or wrong for you. A dichotomy in opinions and thinking reduces everything to something lesser than it is. So, do not think in Binary.

Flaw 2 – Correlation does not always represent causation:

Do not fall prey to false superstitions, biases, and perspectives. Correlation does not mean causation.

Flaw 3– Selective Anecdotes are not evidence:

Looking and focusing your attention only on surviving or success stories is misleading and skews our perspective. You must also try to listen even to failure stories because they are the true hidden treasure of insight.

Flaw 4– The majority is correct:

People like to follow people, even though they are wrong,

and they know it! Do not develop a herd mentality. The majority can be wrong. Our brain is the reason for the Fascinating creatures we are. You must develop and improve critical thinking by overcoming these flaws which hinder your progress.

Habits For Brain And Creativity

Your brain as far as your body goes is the unrivaled organ, and chiefly we are talking about a hundred billion-plus cells that collectively control everything your body does. So, it becomes our responsibility to cultivate a few good habits to keep our brain healthy and increase our creativity.

1. Have Quality Sleep

Chronic lack of sleep puts people at the risk of Alzheimer's disease and other neurological disorders. A continuous lack of sleep harms your memory too. This is because, in your sleep, mechanisms are hard at work relieving you from toxins byproducts that accumulate in your brain throughout the day. So, to avoid these dangerous consequences, develop the habit of having sufficient sleep.

It is advisable to go to sleep as close to 10 PM as you can. Have you ever slept a perfectly reasonable amount like 7 to 9 hours and woke up feeling groggy and tired? The reason is that your body runs on a biological clock that dictates many physiological processes. We have a daily dosage of cortisol in the morning to wake us up and a rise in melatonin at night to put us to sleep. If you can act in sync with this rhythm, falling asleep and getting higher quality sleep is much easier. What our body would prefer for us to do is to fall asleep just a few hours after the sunsets. This differs depending on where in the world you are, but for most people, it is around 10 PM. The powerful anticarcinogen and antioxidant melatonin, as well as the restorative Human Growth Hormone, are secreted mostly between 10 PM and 2 AM. According to Neurologist Kulreet Chaudhary, "If your body is deprived chronically of the regenerative sleep between 10:00 P.M. and 2:00 A.M., then you may still feel tired when you wake up in the morning." Going to sleep around 10 PM is always better.

For example, if you get six hours of sleep from 10 PM to 4 AM, you will feel much better than if you got eight hours of sleep from 1 AM to 9 AM. Improving the quality of sleep overall is incredibly helpful for mood, focus, energy levels, and health in general.

One important point to remember is not to cover your head during sleep. According to research, sleeping with a head beneath the covers can cause brain damage. Some studies indicate that up to twenty-three percent of individuals that sleep with a head covered with the bedsheets develop Dementia and possibly even Alzheimer's. These conditions are in most cases as a result of the lack of enough oxygen to the brain, and so keeping your head free is a useful way of preventing this issue at bay. It is also vital to understand that covering your head as you see means that you'll be re-breathing the air that you breathe out which does not contain a lot of oxygen.

So, make it a habit to sleep as close to 10 pm every day, and never to cover your head during sleep.

2. Limit your usage of a novelty at a click websites

Internet addiction is a real phenomenon, and more and more studies on this topic are coming out. But, you don't have to be technically addicted to see detriments.

Dopamine is the neurotransmitter responsible for making you want to do things and is the reason drugs can be so addictive. Drugs cause a huge surge in dopamine, and when someone becomes overexposed to dopamine, the dopamine receptors downregulate, meaning more dopamine is necessary to get the same amount of motivation. Essentially, the receptors become desensitized. And, it does not have to be surges of dopamine to get you addicted, it can be frequent exposure. For example, the rate of addiction to cigarettes is surprisingly higher than heroin-the difference between the two is you can take a puff of a cigarette and get dopamine to rise dozens of times a day, but you'd be passed out, or dead before you get anywhere near that frequency with heroin. The thing with the internet is that websites like facebook, twitter, Reddit, Imgur, act like that puff of a cigarette. Swipe for a new picture, and you get a bit of dopamine. Scroll down, and you get a bit of dopamine. Click on a link, and you get a bit of dopamine., but you can repeat this hundred of times throughout the day. This will desensitize your dopamine receptors, and it will be harder and harder to get motivated by activities that aren't instantly gratifying. The gap between behavior and reward with the internet is incredibly small - it can be half a second. Behavior: move the thumb. Reward: funny picture. By using the internet too often, it's harder and harder for your brain to tolerate more time between behavior and reward. Imgur can reward you with a funny picture in a couple of seconds, but staying focused on a project can take several hours before getting rewarded with a sense of fulfillment.

3. Exercise Everyday

Get Up and Get Moving. Your body needs physical exercise. Exercise regularly to promote blood flow to your brain that provides growth factors and other good things to brain cells and helps clear away toxins. To exercise 30 minutes a day, 5 days a week, that is a good goal for all of us.

Usually, we look at exercise as mainly just a way to build muscle or lose fat. But exercise has many more benefits. It provides you with impressive mental and physiological benefits too. Exercise has been shown to help people learn much more efficiently, deal with stress in a better way, and drastically reduce anxiety. It improves mood to the point of raising some people out of depression, and it strengthens focus to the point that some ADHD patients prefer to throw out their prescriptions.

A 2007 study found that subjects who did high-intensity exercise beforehand could learn vocabulary words 20% faster than those who remained sedentary. Exercise will also give you more motivation in general.

Earlier, it was explained how excessive use of the internet hampers motivation because it desensitizes your dopamine receptors, making it harder to be motivated by regular activities that do not provide large or frequent releases of dopamine. Well, exercise triggers the creation of new dopamine receptors, meaning you become more sensitive to dopamine, making it easier to be motivated. This will give a boost in willpower and focus on doing the things that you could do, not just the things you want to do now.

4. Stay Hydrated

The importance of Hydration is common knowledge, but most people do not practice this. Water makes up at least 2/3 rd of the human body and plays a vital role in your normal functions, and that's why dehydration can lead to several issues from migraines, constipation, to kidney stones. It can also take on a toll on your brain health, affecting your mood and overall brain function. Symptoms of dehydration include being more prone to irritability, anxiety, and fatigue. Remember that ¾th of the brain is water and when dehydrated, your brain shrinks in volume. According to a study published in 2013 even mild or temporary dehydration can alter your brain function and impact your mood throughout the day which means you are nowhere near the potential performance you could be for that given day resulting in your work and life declining and suffering. The good news is that within 20 minutes of drinking some water, effects such as these are reversed. Dehydration induced headaches are reduced also once you hydrate yourself. So, develop the habit of drinking sufficient water every day into a habit. It is also worth noting that cold water absorbs 20% faster than room-temperature water. So, to increase speedy recovery from dehydration, make sure to drink chilled water as opposed to water at room temperature.

5. Learn Yoga

Yoga is not a mere exercise, and it is the process of discovering your oneness with yourself, the world, and nature. Yoga works on several levels-body, mind, emotion, and energy.
By changing your lifestyle and creating consciousness, it can help you to deal with climatic change, disease prevention, health promotion, and orients you towards comprehensive health.

In yoga practice, you adopt different body postures and patterns that give you the enhanced ability to maintain a specific body position with a firm awareness of your constitutional state for a significant length of time. In ancient times, yoga masters who lived close to nature observed the movement and breathing of animals and birds. Most Yoga poses imitate or represent animals, birds, trees, mountains, etc.

6. Write Your Life Scheme

Do you have a definite life purpose? 98% of people don't.

If you do not understand your life purpose, you remain the walking dead, in a zombie-like state of being. You wander around aimlessly with no destination, no vision. In this state, your life is meaningless.

A life lacking a clear purpose is like traveling without any direction or destination. A life with a clear purpose is akin to driving with a magic GPS.

As it is said, it is not the mountains you must climb that wear you out. It is the little pebble in your shoe.

You have to stop, think, and plan every move forward. Then, Sky is the limit.

Reinvent Yourself

Unleash, awaken your inherent potential lying dormant in you. Create your ideal self. Try to be the person you always cherished to be. Make a fresh start in your life to fulfill your potential.

Why knowing your life purpose is crucial?

Only those who believe in their dreams can fulfill their dreams.

Three pillars in your life:

- Passion - Identify them
- Skill - Harness them
- Opportunities - Look out for them

10 Benefits of having a purpose in life

1. It makes you feel more fulfilled.

2. It makes your life joyous and exciting.

3. It gives you the needed focus and direction.

4. It frees you from unimportant activities.

5. It helps you to gain your success.

6. It boosts your health.

7. It helps you to achieve your goals quicker.

8. It helps you in taking decisions aligned with your purpose of life.

9. It will find your happiness and peace of mind.

10. Yes, you live longer

Tips to live your purpose

- Keep your purpose phrase Short: 12 words maximum. It makes memorizing it easy.

- Keep your purpose simple: No complex words.

- Keep your purpose sound natural.

- Repeat it out loud, a few times a day.

- Keep your purpose illustrated. Associate a picture with your purpose.

  - Step 1: Find an image.
  - Step 2: Add an overlay with your purpose.
  - Step 3: Set it as your screensaver.
  - Step 4: Set it as your phone background

- Keep your purpose visible. Write it down. A simple post like... 'Maximize Potential' will help your brain remember your purpose, and keep your life aligned with it.

- Make sure you build accountability by sharing your aspirations with your near and dear ones. It increases your success prospects by nearly 48%

- Once you are clear of your life's purpose, cherish it, nurture it, and work earnestly to attain grand success in this endeavor.

The technique to pursue:

- Reinvent yourself with positive new traits and habits.

- Reorganize the traits that make you who you are.

- Reprogram yourself to think, speak, and act in ways that will bring about the changes you desire.

- Alter your personality at the very deepest level.

- Interact in the world with greater happiness and added confidence.

- Let go of your past. Build a brighter and better future.

Seven steps for a purposeful life:
- Step 1: Do Something New
- Step 2: Give Time To Yourself
- Step 3: Maintain A Healthy Mind And Body
- Step 4: Prepare To Be Financially Independent
- Step 5: Cultivate A Social Network
- Step 6: Be Positive
- Step 7: Learn

7. Shshshs ....silence, please

A peaceful mind can think better than a worked up mind. So, allow a few minutes of Silence into your mind every day, and see how sharply it helps you to shape and live your life the way you want it to be.

Once, a farmer lost his watch on the farm. He was worried as it had great sentimental value for him. He searched in the barn for a long time. Finally, the dejected farmer gave up. Seeing a group of children playing outside, he decided to take their help in finding his precious watch. He announced that the one who finds the watch would be rewarded. The excited children rushed inside the barn and searched for a long time. However, they too could not find it.

Then one of the boys sought permission to search again, but this time alone. After some time, the boy returned with the missing watch. The happy farmer was greatly surprised and inquired how the boy succeeded. The boy explained, 'Actually, I did not do anything. I sat silently on the ground and listened with attention. In the silence, I could hear the ticking of the watch and traced it.'

The incredible message of this simple story is: The soul knows how to heal itself. Your challenge lies in silencing your Mind.

8. Staying connected to others:

Spare time for socialization. Complex relationships like friendships are suitable for the brain. Health studies show that individuals who are connected socially with family or friend clubs, civic groups or churches have higher levels of certain brain chemicals than socially isolated individuals. The socially isolated individual is much more likely to develop dementia and have a rapid progression of dementia than a person who is socially engaged. Staying socially engaged, staying engaged in conversations stimulates thinking, and boosts language skills. All this is so important to preserving brain health.

9. Follow your heart.

Live your passion. Having found your life plan or purpose, put your whole heart and soul to it. You have to make your own decision, stick to it, and accept the consequences without any complaints.

You can be what you always wanted to be. So, quickly and easily define a brand new you!

10. PPP (Triple P): The path of Patience, Perseverance, and Purity

The triple Ps are the only means to achieve your goal. Achieving a higher goal is a time-consuming affair. Perseverance means continuously putting efforts and energy into the work in hand till it is completed, and the goal is achieved. Impurity brings all kinds of bondages. So, always be pure in your thoughts, words, and deeds.

11. Triple S (SSS) Self-faith, Self Help, Service

Self-faith is believing in one's capacities, abilities, and strength. Action is the mother of self-faith. Start immediately and work on the goal you set for yourself. Life gets a meaning if it is lived for others service expands your heart.

How to Improve Creativity?

Everyone has the potential to be creative. In this section, we will discuss how you can find and develop your inner creativity.

- **Everyone is creative.**

  First, we have to dismiss the notion that anyone anywhere cannot be creative. We have a million brain cells, and they all integrate. Now, anybody with a piece of equipment like that who says I am not creative is making a mistake. What has happened is that they have not been taught how to use that phenomenal piece of equipment.

- **The left and right brain.**

  As we know, the left brain deals with words, numbers, logic, and analysis, and the right brain deals with rhythm, color, shape, form, imagination, and daydreaming. It has been thought that creativity was right-brained, and because it was analyzed wrongly, creativity has been damaged majorly. Creativity needs to use both sides and get the order, the number, the image, the color, the rhythm, the imagination, and the daydreaming all working together.

- **Speed of thought. Speed of thinking**.

It is called fluency. How fast, and rapidly can you generate ideas. And that you can develop by playing at it. You can practice thinking more quickly. You can practice getting those little puzzles and working them out faster, and at a faster speed and that productivity is one of the hallmarks of creative genius.

- **The originality of thought.**

If you were asked, what would you use a coat hanger for and you reply, for hanging a coat, that would not get you high points in creativity? If you said you could use it to fuel a rocketship to the moon by taking the constituent molecules of that particular coat hanger and converting it into some fuel, that's the way out. That is what is known as 'Out of the box thinking.'

- **The flexibility of thought.**

Most people tend to focus on one way and say "this

is the way I think," "this is the way I see that" when it should be how many ways can you see that, from how many perspectives can you look at it from. And the great creative thinkers play with looking at different perspectives.

- **Imagination and Association.**

  All great creative thinkers are using their imagination. What they are doing, in addition to that is that they are making links between things. So, they are associating. S, it is Imagination and Association. The two significant keywords for creativity and what you have to do when you are being creative is to find those associations and connections between things that are going to create something new.

Change Your Life with Powerful Habits

Small hinges open big doors. At first, it might not seem like you are accomplishing much, but don't be disappointed or fooled. Here are the powerful habits which strengthen your confidence and help you get whatever you want in life.

- **Walking**

  Throughout the day, your mind is filled with diverse thoughts. You overlook your immediate surroundings while blindly going through the daily motions. Walking is a time to slow down, to immerse yourself in the environment while relaxing into the pace of nature. Walking is not a destination guided activity. It is a rejuvenating activity where you focus on each moment as it comes rewarding you with greater physical awareness. You are attentive to the slightest change in your mental state.

Enjoy your walk. Take care to wear comfortable clothes and footwear. A morning walk instills energy and focuses throughout the day. An evening walk may be an excellent way to unwind, providing you a chance to relax before sleep.

Walk at a languid pace, paying attention to your breathing. When you focus on the slow and steady breath, it will allow your feet to slow down as well. When you come across flowers, take a moment to inhale their scent, letting the fragrance enliven you to the moment. Noticing all of these enchanting things will allow you to relax and absorb yourself in the present moment completely. Breathe from the abdomen and relax your legs and torso.

As you walk, let your mind flow with your body.

Allow your mind to consciously scan the body and notice all the sensations you feel as you walk. Notice how your feet contact the ground and carry you with steady sureness. You will lose yourself in a meditative state as you become more and more observant. Walking reinforces a positive mental attitude powerfully. Walking balances your nervous system and initiates the relaxation response.

- **Splash cold water** on your head and face when bathing. This stimulates blood flow to the brain. You feel more energetic.

- **Give up Tendencies to think in a certain way.** Become flexible to implement new ways of thinking. Be more proactive in new learning. Adopt novel ways to deal with available information. Give up the stereotyped thought process. Be innovative and open to new thought processes.

- **Focus on the data:** In situations that demand decision making, focus on the evidence or information. It takes a little bit of effort. Once this becomes a habit, it's nearly effortless.

- **Seek out contrary data and conclusions:** Such knowledge building is at the core of the scientific investigation.

- **Understand the noise:** Focus on the vital aspect at hand. Filter out all unnecessary noise that is of no use to you. Noise is useful when you learn to avoid background information correctly.

- **Test and Retest:** Do not hurry to conclude. Be consistent, patient, and non-judgemental.

- **Make educated guesses:** It helps as it is from your rich knowledge-base.

- **Avoid distractions and misattributions: Do not give into** attention diverters. Be focussed.

- **Have Multiple Perspectives:** You can look at a situation from another point of view or a different angle. In both cases, you will get new information. Your opinions could change. It is easier to think from somebody else's perspective than to think from an imaginary perspective. For example, flying can be thought of from a pilot's point of view, or a passenger's, or the technical assistant's point of view.

- **Accept that you don't know what you don't know:** In many situations, it is not possible to understand the clockwork that leads to a phenomenon.

- **Develop a richer thinking vocabulary** and practice brain teasers.

- **Fiction reading and watching Sci-Fi**, over-the-top, exaggerated outlandishly ridiculous stuff stimulates your creative talent too.

- **Learn different languages culturally**. One example is English speakers learning Russian. Try to learn two diverse languages simultaneously instead of one at a time. Comparing and contrasting between 2 languages (or any two concepts) helps you learn them faster.

- **Stretch your Thought Spectrum**. Ask a question. Think of and generate not one, but five different answers to the question.

- **Get creative by overcoming functional fixedness**. Try to make all the tools multipurpose. Come out of the ridiculous notion that an object can only be used in one way.

- **Practice thinking about the same thing at different times in a day.** When you think about the same subject at different times, the pause between 2-time slots of the same thought greatly influences how the thought manifests.

- **Change your perspective**. Physically and metaphorically. This often adds new insight. Ask questions of all kinds, no matter how obvious or silly they sound.

- **Develop a Friend's Vision.** *It is* bringing in other people in your thinking like How would Alice do this?

- **Expand your skillset**. Spend your leisure time learning a new language, a new recipe, music, make-up, food, game, videography, etc.

- **Spend some quality time to train your mind and body:** Practice the following points: Be practical and try to act on things instead of overthinking about anything or anyone which you can't control.

- **Sleep like a log:** Sleep is your most significant learning activity. It enhances short term and long term learning and memory. Proper sleep and power naps do wonder for your brain: Try to get at least 6–7 hours sleep at night and during daytime; whenever you feel sleepy, take a 15 to 20 mins power. It is not a luxury. It is common sense. It energizes you making you fresher, concentrated during your work, and more productive.

- **Prioritize your work:** Pay attention to and do things first, which is most important to you, now, and in the long run.

- **Develop A Positive Attitude:** Try to see the bright side, even of bad situations. Viewing the situation as a **challenge** helps you to mobilize your resources and allows you to achieve a situation more easily while viewing the same situation as a **threat** can lead to a greater tendency to feel stressed and shut down.

- **Choose Your Friends Wisely:** Always try to surround yourself with people who motivate you, who stay with you in good and bad times, who add value to your life, and who help you in your personal and professional life. Frequently meet with your good old friends who know you better and talk about those best days, their life, and work.

- **Try To Enjoy Every Second Of Your Life:** Take

pleasure from the small and sweet things in life. Money cannot always bring happiness. Sometimes, small good things make our day.

- **Make Good Resolutions If You Need Them**: Do not make it for an entire month or a year, but make it for 5 to 10 days at a time. When you succeed, repeat it for the next set of 5 or 10 days. Very soon, it becomes your habit!

- **Never Be Pessimistic. Do Not Regret Anything:** If you get an opportunity, you grab it. Try to make the best use of every single opportunity that comes your way. There are no failures in life; only life lessons learned.

- **Take A Holiday For Yourself:** Pamper yourself now and then. Do not limit yourself to your city, workplace, and home. Explore new places.

- **Be A Good Human Being And A Kind Hearted Person:** Always try to help others who are in need. Do it as a duty towards your fellow beings. It will make them happy, and you will feel good. Never miss a chance to appreciate others' good work!

- **Create Social Bonds With A Variety Of People:** Come out of your shell. Make new friends in your community at your workplace. Be amicable and helpful to all the people you come across.

- **Remember to Remember**: This is the easiest, proven, and profound technique to improve your brain health. You remind yourself that this is vital information and must recall it later. This strengthens and bolsters the circuits that the brain uses for that information. The information could be speech, landmarks, test answers, etc.

- **Lifestyle Modifications**: Having adequate amounts of Vitamin B 12 is associated with a good memory. Another study reveals that exercising four hours after studying consolidates memory better than immediate exercise.

- **Learn To Code**: Different processes like graphical representation, calculations, string manipulation, file conversion, automation of simple tasks, machine learning, web crawling, etc. greatly influence your thinking. This influence is fruitful with the conscious application of it.

- **Learn statistics**: It is one of the systematic, most productive, and surest ways to acquire new ways of thinking. You can better understand what information is essential and what isn't. The normal distribution teaches you what can be expected. How big an influence or contribution something has, has been clearly explained by the Pareto principle. Probability teaches you how likely something is.

- **Imitate Animal Behavior**: Look at bees, ants, birds, snakes, etc. Observe them and learn how animals do certain things. Apply a similar principle in your thinking. This brings more variety to how you think and act. Imitation helps to improve your subconscious mind power, it boosts your innate memory, enhances your recall faculty, sharpens your study attention span, and inspires you to learn more and assimilate more information.

- **Add variety to what you learn and how you learn:** The main prerequisite for adaptive learning is Variance –While trying to solve a problem – don't look for a direct solution. Break down the problem into smaller chunks, and then try to solve each problem. Seek help if you can't solve something smaller.

- **Give yourself a chance to solve**: The brain is active in processing information all the time. The answer may come to you. Your accomplishment in giving yourself time and solving a problem is a big reward to motivate you.

- **The Healing Power of Pets:** There are moments in your life when you feel isolated and alone. Several studies have found that a few minutes a day petting an animal lowers Cortisol, the stress hormone, and increases Serotonin, the feel-good hormone. Pets are suitable for your overall health and well-being, including brain health. The beautiful results are lowered heart rates and blood pressure and decreased depression.

- **Practice Radical forgiveness:** One of the things you can do immediately without any pricey machinery is 'Radical Forgiveness.' Radical forgiveness is the key to the healthiest brain state. Radical forgiveness is one of the biggest things that you can bring into your life. Forgive yourself or someone else who hurt you every single day.

- **Branch Out:** Engage in outdoor and indoor sports and cultural activities. Shared hobbies are a great way to meet and develop friendships with like-minded people. Become a volunteer or join neighborhood clubs. You'll be surprised at how good it makes you feel.

- **Brain-Body Workout:** Do not forget the brain-body workout. Your brain gets an extra flow of blood every time you work out. This oxygen-rich blood helps to preserve the brain. Studies show that individuals who exercise regularly have less brain shrinkage over time than those who don't. Exercise programs should last at least 30 minutes to get the most benefit concerning brain function. Programs that combine strength training with aerobic exercise are most effective.

  A 2014 Harvard Health letter said that exercise helps memory in both direct and indirect ways. It helps directly because exercise reduces inflammation – and that helps your brain, and it encourages the growth of new blood cells in the brain. And indirectly, exercise is going to help your memory because it is going to help you sleep better, and also help to reduce your stress and anxiety. And that is going to help your memory.

- **Good Chemistry:** Thank good chemistry. Your consciousness, your memory functions, and your emotions all depend on minor fluctuations and brain chemicals. You may feel depressed, anxious for a host of other emotions that can make life difficult if your brain chemistry is off. So, if you are feeling anxious or depressed, seek medical care. You may not only feel better; you will also be able to perform at your mental best.

Prepare "To Do" Lists: Write Post-it notes, set the alarm, and leave items, such as keys, stationery items, glasses, and wallet in the same place every day. If you're troubled by financial issues, for example, develop a detailed plan to reduce your expenses and debt.

Develop These Pristine Qualities:

- Appreciate when others win.

- Work diligently to see ideas come to fruition

- Be a Meta thinker.

- Prefer making and enhancing rules

- Believing nothing is sacred or a sin.

- Love solving problems.

- Great at self-assessment

- Create your future self.

- Believe you are in total control.

- Do everything with intent.

- Do not let your ego suffer when you fail.

- Act in spite of limitations

9 Damaging Habits To Keep At Bay:

Some habits are sure to fill your life with unhappiness. Identify them and show them the door if you want to lead a happy life.

1. **Suppressing your feelings within**

   The great misconceptions concerning Emotional Intelligence (EQ) is that it is assumed that we must repress our true feelings and holding them in. Though it is true that high EQ individuals do not exhibit mood swings or allow their temper to erupt on impulse, we must get the basics right. Emotional intelligence means honoring your feelings and allowing yourself to develop a calm mindset, which helps you reap good returns in your personal and professional life. It helps you to reach your goals.

2. **Being a slave to technology**

   We were taught to love people and use things. Unfortunately, today, we are loving things and using people. We are in a trap of modern technology. We are so obsessed with our gadgets that we become oblivious to reality. Our virtual world has replaced our real world.

3. **Spending more time and effort to acquire possessions.**

The Law of Diminishing Utility works when we seek happiness by acquiring worldly possessions and wealth. Many studies made across the globe showed that people living in extreme poverty experienced a significant increase in happiness when their financial circumstances improved. However, their happiness dropped off quickly above the annual income of $20,000. So, the stark reality is money does not bring happiness. It is a means of keeping you comfortable and secure. Material things do not and cannot keep you happy. When you compete with others, making a habit of chasing things, you are likely to remain unhappy because true happiness and worldly fortunes are inversely related.

4. **Waiting for the future**

Do not fix a future date to be happy telling yourself, "I'll be happy when ..." Happiness is your true nature and your birthright. Just by removing the veil of ignorance and with awareness, you can bask in the glory never-ending state of happiness and bliss. So, focus on being happy right now, in the present moment because the tomorrow of your dreams may never come.

5. Give up Fighting change

Be prepared for change. Never try to avoid change. Change is an inevitable part of life; a natural process that allows you to grow into a better person. If you do not change, you stagnate. It is a significant barrier you cannot surmount. There are many things in life which are beyond our control. So, see change as a challenge, and not as a threat.

So, anticipate change and understand your options if changes occur. This protects you from intense negative emotions that grip you like surprise, fear, shock, and disappointment when an unforeseen situation and changes happen around you.

6. Pessimism

Pessimism is the burning fuel for unhappiness. A pessimistic attitude is akin to a self-fulfilling prophecy. If you expect bad things, you are inviting bad things into your life. Pessimistic thoughts are tough to shake off until you pay attention to the intention to ward off and recognize how illogical they are.

7. Trying to keep up with the peers

Envy and jealousy are incompatible with happiness. You must not wish to or try to live like others. Do you want your life to be an original masterpiece or a poor imitation? Every one of us is distinct and different in many ways. So, if you are in the habit of constantly comparing yourself with others, it's time to stop. An interesting observation from a study was that most subjects said they are OK with making less money, provided everybody else did, too. This kind of thinking is wrong. Wish for your good and others welfare also. Always remember that we are all interconnected, and in others happiness lies your true happiness.

8. Waiting for miracles to happen, not improving

Life is not a fairytale story. Do not have a laid back attitude. Even God helps those who help themselves. Do not wait for someone to make things better for you. Instead of proactive, start setting goals, learning, and improving yourself.

9. Staying Home

When you are feeling down and sad, you are tempted to avoid other people. This is a huge blunder. Come out of your home. Connect with Nature. Mingle with others. When you feel unhappy, it is good to socialize, even when you do not enjoy it.

Changing your habits is one of the best things that you can do for yourself. This way, you can take control of your happiness makings everyone around you happier, too.

Unlock Your Potential: The Key To Creating Positive Habits

Install these 3 Free Apps to Track Your Progress

1. **Perspective Daily Journal.**

It is user-friendly. It provides users greater insight and self-awareness. In this journaling app, entries can be viewed across a "life calendar" timeline. This helps you to draw connections between your past, present, and future activities.

2. **Day One Journal.**

An ideal alternative to paper and pencil, this app makes journaling easy with its elegant and effective reminders and interface.

3. **Dream Journal Ultimate.**

As the name suggests, you log your dreams, and the app analyzes them for common themes and compares them to similar dreams from people around the world.

10 Habits You Must Drop

1. Saying 'Yes' always

2. Hanging Onto People Who Don't Want to Grow

3. Working Through Lunch. It lowers your overall productivity and leads to burnout faster.

4. Failing to Exercise

5. Multitasking

6. Pinging People

7. Striving for Perfection

8. Not Protecting Your Recharge Time

9. Immediately Answering PMs and Emails

10. Spending your day without assigning priorities

4 Taboo List:

1. Don't whine and blame others.

2. Don't sit still.

3. Don't be unfocused.

4. Don't overestimate your talent.

Never

1. Return to what hasn't worked.

2. Do anything that requires you to be someone you are not.

3. Try to change another person.

4. Believe you can please everyone.

5. Choose short-term comfort over long-term benefit.

6. Trust someone or something that appears flawless.

7. Take your eyes off the big picture.

8. Fail to ask why you are where you find yourself.

Chapter 9: Nourish Your Brain

You only have one brain. Protect it NOW.

Food for Brain

You can increase your brain health and brain by making a few changes in your food habits and food ingredients. Add to your menu the food items that increase your focus, concentration, mental clarity, and memory. What you need to do is to reduce and diminish the regular sources of energy your brain habitually uses for fuel as this food limits your brain's real capacity. As an alternative, you must tap into the brain's preferred source of energy which is generally covered up and locked away due to our faulty diets and bad eating habits. By making some adjustments to these habits, you will be able to fuel your brain with another source of energy, which allows it to run up to 70 percent more efficiently than it would typically do so. You must feed your brain with this hidden super fuel. It unlocks your true brain power and capacity.

So, the first thing you have to do is to put aside and forget about a regular food pyramid. Your food generally comprises more of carbohydrates. You try to limit your intake of fats. During digestion, your body will break down carbohydrates, and excess protein into sugar known as glucose, and that glucose will force its way as the first source of energy for both your brain and body, leaving other better sources of energy untapped and all that excess glucose will be converted into stored fat. So, this way of eating will necessarily make you fat and stupid, so flip that food pyramid upside down, and instead, eat the majority of your caloric intake in fat while keeping the carbohydrates extremely low. This will not make you gain weight and become fat unless you eat extreme amounts of course, but pretty much, the opposite will make you into a fat-burning machine that uses that fat as the primary source of fuel as blood sugar and glucose are depleted from the lack of carbohydrates. This is generally known as Ketogenic diet and requires you to get 70 to 80 percent of your caloric intake from fat, 15 to 20 percent from protein, and inevitably some carbohydrates. You are now making use of that preferred source of energy, and instead of storing fat, you are currently using that fat as energy, and when that fat is broken down, ketone bodies are released to energize the brain. Studies have shown that the brain can run up to 70 percent more efficiently on ketone instead of glucose. So, this new way of eating will necessarily make you energetic and smart.

Forget about many small meals a day. You must start eating fewer and larger meals. This way, you fast for a large part of the day, very close to 16 hours. This gives you an 8-hour eating window period. This brings about many mental and physical benefits. Intermittent fasting helps your body to build up the depletion of glucose and fuel the brain using ketones. This will increase your memory, ability to remember, focus, and concentration. This concurrently reduces the risk of Parkinson's disease and Alzheimer's. It increases the brain-derived neurotrophic factor (the BDNF,), to 400 percent. This activates stem cells of the brain that make new nerves, neurons, and brain cells. And BDNF is also highly involved in your muscles and appears to be a huge reason why a physical workout has such an impact on your brain and fasting improves neuroplasticity, which is essential for learning and memory improvement. As the brain ages, it tends to become less neoplastic and intermittent fasting prevents this, and you will be able to have significant mental clarity even as you get older. It enhances gene regulation. It activates Vitae genes, the repair genes whose main function is to delay the aging process. As Vitagenes are activated, there is a significant decrease in the occurrence of age-related diseases. It improves your health and prolongs your life span.

Brainy Dose:

Recommended foods: Food plays a significant role in boosting short-term and long-term brain function and maintain concentration.

The foods you eat affect your mood, your brain energy, your memory, and even your ability to handle stress, complex problems, or simple daily tasks. Eating a brain-boosting diet can support the structure and health of your brain. This also enhances your overall physical, mental, and emotional health.

Your brain is an energy-intensive vital organ, using about 20 percent of your body's calories. Your brain works more sharply if your diet includes more nutrients. So, give it plenty of good fuel to function efficiently throughout the day.

Like your body, the brain also needs Omega-3 fatty acids that help build and repair brain cells. Antioxidants which reduce cellular stress and inflammation, and which are linked to brain aging and neurodegenerative disorders, such as Alzheimer's disease are also needed by your brain.

All these wonderful foods keep your memory, attention, speed, focus, and creativity as sharp as it can be.

Best brain foods:

1. Oily fish

Oily fish like salmon, Mackerel, Tuna, Herring, Sardines, which are a good source of omega-3 fatty acids boost brain function, better cognition, or thinking abilities. They help build membranes around each cell in the body, including the brain cells. They, thus improve the structure of brain cells called neurons.

A study conducted in 2017 found that people with high levels of omega-3s had increased blood flow in the brain.

2. Dark chocolate

Dark chocolate contains cocoa (cacao) that contains antioxidant flavonoids. It helps combat oxidative stress, which leads to age-related cognitive decline and brain diseases.

It encourages neuron and blood vessel growth in the brain parts involved in learning. They also stimulate blood flow in the brain and improve your memory power.

3. Berries

Many berries like strawberries, blackberries, blueberries, strawberries, black currants, mulberries are rich in antioxidants like flavonoid, anthocyanin, caffeic acid, catechin, and quercetin. The antioxidant compounds in berries have several positive effects on the brain.

- Improvement in communication between brain cells
- Better memory, enhanced learning, and improved cognitive functions.
- Augments verbal comprehension, numerical ability, reasoning, and decision making.
- Reduce inflammation throughout the body
- Increase neural plasticity. This helps brain cells to form new connections, thus, boosting memory and learning.
- Delay aging-related neurodegenerative diseases and cognitive decline

4. Nuts and seeds

Nuts and seeds are a plant-based source of healthful fats proteins and resveratrol. Soybeans, nuts, flaxseed, almond and sunflower seeds, hazel seeds, canola oils, cashews, and flaxseed, Chia seeds, walnuts, peanuts, and Brazil nuts are also rich sources for omega-3 fatty acids and antioxidants. A 2014 study found that eating more nuts and seeds, which are high in vitamin E contributed to better brain function, improved cognition, and reduced risk of Alzheimer's disease.

5. Whole grains

Eating whole grains like brown rice, barley, oatmeal, whole-grain bread, whole-grain pasta are excellent sources of antioxidants.

6. Coffee

We usually drink coffee to stay awake, boost alertness, enhance concentration, and focus. The caffeine in coffee blocks adenosine in the brain called, which makes a person feel sleepy. According to a 2018 study, caffeine causes an increase in brain entropy activity, which increases the brain's capacity for processing information. Coffee is also a source of antioxidants that support brain health as you get older. A recent study has linked lifelong coffee consumption with reduced risk of cognitive decline, stroke, Parkinson's disease, Alzheimer's disease, etc.

7. Avocados

High Avocados are an excellent source of healthy unsaturated fat. This reduces blood pressure and may lower the risk of cognitive decline.

8. Eggs

Eggs can be an effective brain food as they are a good source of vitamin B-6, vitamin B-12, and folic acid. It prevents brain shrinkage and delays cognitive decline.

9. Legumes

Leafy greens are the supreme source of carbohydrates, mainly complex carbohydrates. The complex carbohydrates found in legumes are also very rich in fiber. Fiber is known to slow down absorption, provide a steady supply of glucose to the brain. Moreover, it significantly minimizes the risks of sugar spikes common with many other traditional sugar sources.

10. **Kale**

Also known as a superfood, Kale may support brain health as it contains vital antioxidants like glucosinolates, and other vitamins and minerals.

11. **Mint**

Mint is a rich source of Vitamin A, and also Vitamin C. Vitamin A can help boost learning skills and increase brain plasticity, while Vitamin C is known to protect against cognitive decline. According to a study, consumption of mint and even the scent of mint positively affects the functioning of the brain. It boosts memory and mental alertness. It also helps improve your necessary clerical skills, such as typing and memorization.

12. **Broccoli**

Broccoli and other cruciferous vegetables like

Brussel sprouts, bok Choy, cabbage, cauliflower, turnips are rich in fiber and nutrients. Broccoli is reputed to be the best food to improve your memory and boost your brainpower. It is rich in calcium, Vitamin B, beta carotene, iron, fiber, and Vitamin K. It is rich in glucosinolates. When the body breaks these down, they produce isothiocyanates that protect against free radicals. Broccoli maintains proper blood circulation and plays a significant role in removing heavy metals that cause major brain damage. Broccoli is rich in potassium. This high potassium content helps the nervous system and the brain. Research results also suggest that cauliflower and Broccoli play a significant role and aids the brain in healing itself after an injury.

It reduces oxidative stress and lowers the risk of neurodegenerative diseases. Broccoli is also a rich source of vitamin C and flavonoids that can further boost a person's brain health.

13. **Beets**

You can increase your brain power naturally by including more beets in your staple diet. Beets are rich in Nitrates. Nitrates enhance the brain's executive functioning as nitrates increase the blood flow to the parts of the brain related to the brain's executive functions. Beets are a rich source of Vitamin B9. Vitamin B9 aids in improving the brain's cognitive functioning and plays a pivotal role in delaying dementia. Also, beets are rich in Carotenoids, the fat-soluble pigments, which can help in boosting brain functioning and fight depression.

14. Coconut Oil

It contains medium-chain triglycerides that raise the levels of beneficial HDL cholesterol in the body. Your body uses medium-chain triglycerides for energy, leaving glucose, the primary source of fuel for the brain. It is also found to have a beneficial effect on blood sugar, blood pressure, and cholesterol. Whatever food is good for the heart and blood circulation is also good for the Brain. Coconut oil also has anti-inflammatory properties. Research studies have shown that coconut oil helps to prevent memory-related diseases like Dementia and Alzheimer's.

Supplements to enhance brain function

Brain-boosting foods are the ones that contain one or more of the following:

- Antioxidants, such as flavonoids, or vitamin E
- B vitamins
- Healthy fats
- Omega fatty acids

Food Tips:

- **Veg out**

  Increase your intake of fruits and vegetables and reduce the amount of meat and animal products that you consume. The brain requires a proper mixture of nutrients to be healthy. Five servings of fruits and vegetables a day can help you keep your brain healthy, and your memory sharp.

- **Monitor your salt intake.**

  Salt levels in your body affect your memory. When your diet is deficient in salt, it can hurt your short-term memory. But if you go overboard and have too much salt, that is not good for your memory and has even been linked to Alzheimer's disease.

- **Avoid excessive sugar**

The hippocampus is a part of your brain, which is very sensitive to sugar. The hippocampus plays a vital role in learning, memory, and long-term memory. It even plays a role in Alzheimer's disease and depression. So, avoid excessive sugar for better memory.

- **Avoid excessive alcohol**

If you take alcohol and memorize at the same time, it not only hurts your memory in the current short-term memory, but it also has very damaging effects in your long-term memory over time.

- **Moderate consumption of alcohol is suitable for your memory**

Small amounts of alcohol, and maybe having a glass of wine every day is good for your memory.

Chapter 10: Exercises and Memory Improvement Techniques

10 Brain Exercises That Boost Memory:

Trying to learn new things, exploring new avenues and thinking differently are the best ways to improve brain health.

With time, we lose not only muscle, but our brain too is subject to atrophy. Your brain's cognitive reserve, in particular, degenerates. It gradually loses its ability to withstand neurological damage due to aging and other factors. This manifests as visible signs of slowing or memory loss as you grow older day by day. Your speed and accuracy in performing physical and mental tasks diminish over time.

In 2013, a systematic and most detailed study was made to establish the connection between a person's lifestyle and dementia risk. The result of the study was interesting. The researchers found that people who participate in multiple health behaviors significantly reduce their risk of dementia. The results of this 2013 study, were published in PLOS

ONE. The study covered 2,235 men for 30 years. Their participation in five healthy lifestyle behaviors was measured. The health parameters were:

- Non-smoking
- Optimal BMI
- High fruit and vegetable intake
- Regular physical activity
- Low to moderate alcohol intake.

The participants in the study who followed at least four or all five of the behaviors were 60 percent less likely to develop dementia and cognitive impairment.

Some researchers believe that people who pay less attention to the things around them are more vulnerable and suffer from dementia. For this reason, relatively passive and sedentary activities, such as playing video games, being glued to the mobile, sitting in front of a TV for hours together can be detrimental to brain health over time.

Working Models:

Today, in the age of the Internet, we find many brain training software everywhere. Do these brain training software improve your brain health? They are yet to show any significant neurological benefits for older adults. The results of an elaborate study were published in a 2014 review, and published in PLOS Medicine. Researchers in Australia made 52 different studies on computerized cognitive training for a total of 4,885 participants found that the games are not particularly useful in improving brain performance.

You must engage in novel and challenging brain exercises that strengthen your brain function. Your daily newspaper is a rich storehouse for different brain games. You can try solving simple, exciting games like Sudoku and word games. Comic strips are not only engaging but also increases our attention span and cognitive ability.

Simple ways to do things differently are:

- Drive home via a different route
- Brush your teeth with your opposite hand.

Simple Exercises for a sharp, fit, and healthy brain:

1. **Test your recall.** Every morning as soon as you wake up, make a list of things to do, groceries to buy, people to meet, emails to send, bills to pay, meetings to attend, friends to meet, just anything else that

comes to mind and memorize it. Put the paper away. After an hour or so, try to recollect as many items you can recall. With practice, you must be able to remember more and more items. You can get the most significant mental stimulation by adding more and more challenging items on the list.

2. **Add more music to your life.** Researches stand testimony to the fact that learning anything complex and new over a prolonged period is ideal for nourishing the aging mind.

3. **Put the calculator away.** Try to work out calculations without the aid of a calculator, pencil, and paper, or computer.

4. **Try new recipes.** Cooking is a complete brain stimulator as while cooking; we use all the senses, namely sight, touch, smell, and taste. Cooking uses brain faculties.

5. **Learn a new language.** Listening, uttering, and writing a new language stimulates the brain. When you develop a rich vocabulary, it reduces the risk of cognitive decline.

6. **Draw a memory map.** When you visit new places, after returning home, try to draw a map of the area.

7. **Activate your taste buds.** When eating, try to be conscious of the flavors of the several individual

ingredients in your meal like sweet, sour, salty, bitter, subtle herbs, and spices.

8. **Reinforce your hand-eye coordination.** Hobbies such as drawing, painting, knitting, Rubix's cube, assembling a puzzle, etc. involves fine-motor skills which keep your brain hale and healthy.

9. **Practice Heart-head-hand associated activities** such as yoga, golf, or tennis keeps you fit, enthusiastic, and your brain charged.

Just as we can prevent heart disease by taking certain precautions, we can keep our brain healthy by doing simple exercises that keep your brain alert, active, and smart.

Win the Chopstick Challenge and Increase your mental focus:

We use a fork and knife to eat our food. In some countries, they use the right hand, and in some others like Japan, China, Vietnam, Korea, and Taiwan. So, for non- chopstick users, eating with chopsticks is a challenge. Eating noodles with Chopsticks may not appear a big challenge, but what about eating peas using Chopsticks? Yes, this is a challenge for sure.

Marvelous benefits as supported by scientific studies:

Benefit 1: Franklin University has given scientific evidence that when you perform a novel task like trying to eat with chopsticks,

- Your brain is tested and often grows new brain cells to help you memorize.
- Installs the new ability being learned.
- Activates brain cells.

Benefit 2: When you eat food in small portions or bites, it helps you digest your food better, which, in turn, gives you more potential energy.

Benefit3: To eat with chopsticks also means you take smaller mouthfuls of food. This gives you more time to chew your food, eat lesser portions, and also it is easier to digest.

This proves that the brain is actively involved when you engage in challenging tasks. This fun-filled activity helps you with not one, but in many ways. So, challenge yourself, it works wonders for your brain health and power.

The Human Potential Tree:

The Story of the Chinese Bamboo Tree.

The Chines Bamboo Tree, like all plants, needs fertile soil, sunlight, and water to grow. No visible activity is noticed in the first, the second, the third, and the fourth year. We start wondering if our patience and our efforts will ever be rewarded. Finally, in the fifth year, you behold, a miracle! You see unbounded growth; an astounding grows to 80 feet in six weeks!

Though superfluously, it appears that the Chinese Bamboo Tree was not growing at all for four years, and has grown exponentially in the fifth. The fact is that the little tree was throughout the years, growing underground all the time. Just as a caterpillar grows into a beautiful butterfly after an intense struggle inside a cocoon, we too must go through the struggle phase before we manifest our goals.

Change takes time and effort. It's slow and steady in showing any progress. But it is a prerequisite for growth. You need to have tons of patience and persistence.

Chapter 11: Nurture A Success Mindset

Develop a Sense of Purpose and Mission for Your Life. This way, it is much easier to let go of anything that distracts or takes time away from it.

The Thought Sifter: Your Beliefs Strengthen or Weaken Your Motivation

A person with a **fixed mindset**, believe that traits like talent, creativity, intelligence are largely static and predetermined by your upbringing and genes and that they cannot do anything about it. A person with a **growth mindset** believes that new skills and talent can be learned in life. This is vindicated by the results of scientific studies. A growth mindset helps you achieve your goals even during adverse times.

The Art And Science Of Perseverance

We are the creators of our destiny. Life gets a meaning when lived with a purpose and mission. So, **persevere.**

Let us now look into the lives of path makers:

The message they give us is- **Yes, you can**

Inspiring Lives

Helen Keller:

The name Helen Keller is known all over the world as a symbol of bravery and courage. She was a woman with radiant intelligence, great achievements, and high ambition who dedicated her life to helping others.

Helen Keller, at birth, was a healthy child. She was very active and began walking at the age of 1.

In 1882, Helen suffered from brain fever. She lost her sight and hearing capabilities at the age of 19 months old. To give her proper training, Anne Sullivan was appointed as her teacher. This teacher and pupil relationship lasted for 49 years.

The first word she taught was "doll' to help Helen to understand the gift she bought for her. She worked hard for 25 years to learn to speak.

In 1896, the public came to know about her story, and she started to meet famous and influential people. She wrote her autobiography *'The Story of My Life.'*

After completing her college, she started working on behalf of other handicapped people. She worked enthusiastically for the welfare of visually challenged people.

She is remembered even today with great admiration for her very inspiring and remarkable life.

Stephen William Hawking

Exactly after 300 years of the death of Galileo, on 8th January 1942, Stephen William Hawking was born in Oxford, England. At the age of 8, he moved with his family to St. Albans, a town about 20 miles away from the north of London. His father wanted him to do medicine, but Stephen preferred to study mathematics.

When he was doing his formal study of cosmology, he had Lou Gehrig's disease. Though he used a wheelchair and was dependent on a computerized voice system for all communication, yet Stephen lived a balanced life, continued to combining his research in theoretical physics with life. He gave several public lectures. He experienced the incredible weightlessness in the year 2007 with the aid of Zero-G Corporation, and he always hoped to be in space one day. His life goal was to study the marvels of the universe.

On 14 March 2018, Stephen Hawking passed away aged 76

Stephen King

How Stevie Became a Best Selling Author and a Millionaire?

Stevie, since childhood, wanted to be a writer. He wrote his first story when he was just twelve. His mother liked his work and sent his story to a magazine very confident that it will be published. However, it was rejected. Stevie was not disheartened. He kept on writing. He placed the rejection letter prominently on his bedroom wall. By the time he crossed his teens, he had an extensive collection of rejection letters.

Stevie was now 26-year-old school teacher with a family of a wife and two children. One fine day, he received a telegram from the publishing house Doubleday publishing. They proposed to publish Stevie's first novel – a horror fiction story about a teenage girl Carrie White, who had telekinetic powers. He got an advance for it. Very soon, *Carrie* earned him four hundred thousand dollars. Stephen King became a renowned writer.

They all succeeded due to their choice to persevere. The age-old saying is, 'Successful people don't do different things. They do things differently,' and that makes all the difference.

Chapter 12: Brain Reset

A Simple Strategy With A Big Impact

Just watching your brain for only five minutes will leave you stupefied. You will be amazed at how your brain does several complex tasks for you like cognition, understand, process, analyze, retrieve, and memorize. There is a continuous stream of hundreds of thoughts crossing your mind every day.

As long as your brain is healthy, you are physically and mentally sound. However, when your brain is disturbed, restless, and stressed out, your daily routine will fall apart, and life becomes a misery.

However, your brain can be reset and reorganized. Change Your Mindset. By altering your thinking, you can alter your life.

Changing a mental habit requires a deliberate choice and takes dedication, time, and practice. - Thoreau

Are You Willing To Change?

Change is a prerequisite to give up a bad habit, form a new habit, modify behavior, come up with an innovative idea.

You Must Know How To Change?

Neuroscience confirms that you can bring effective and sustainable changes following a few proven steps that center on thinking.

The 4 R's:

Neuropsychiatrists, in association with the UCLA School of Medicine, developed a successful non-drug behavior therapy for patients suffering from obsessive-compulsive disorder (OCD), the most locked up form of behavior.

Step 1. Relabel

The first step is to relabel each thought that crosses your mind, your every feeling, or general behavior with a new name or tag. You can relabel an unwanted thought as "brain glitch." or "false message."

Step 2. Reattribute

You must be aware of and recognize the undesired thoughts that occur frequently. You must ask yourself, "Why are these disturbing old thoughts coming back to me again and again?" Now that you know it is a false message, you must think about what you can do about it.

Step 3. Refocus

It is the most challenging step. It needs a lot of grit, commitment, and willpower. It is tough work as it initiates actual behavior changes. You have to start afresh. You must learn a new behavior, giving up your habitual behavior. It creates a new you. It is a process of new learning and de-learning at the same time. When you put yourself into this chosen mold with great enthusiasm, enjoy doing it, and do it consistently every time, magic is bound to happen. Slowly and steadily, you are intentionally and consciously creating new patterns, new mindsets. By refusing to be misled by the old, habituated messages, by understanding they are not in your best interest, you are naturally in charge of your brain, regulating, and controlling it. With practice, it will bear the desired fruits.

Step 4. Revalue

With awareness and consistent effort, you are replacing the old behavior with the new ones. You are now viewing old patterns as simple distractions you can overcome. They are of little value. You now devalue them as entirely worthless. When they lose weight and intensity, eventually, the old thoughts begin to fade away and get slowly erased from your memory.

These four steps will undoubtedly help lead a fulfilling life.

Micro Novelties: We only use 10 percent of our brain. Our brain thrives on new and novel ideas. Add as many novel ideas as you can to your daily life. Here are three 'micro novelties' to include in your life.

Learn A Language Or Music:

Along with giving you immense joy, learning to play

a musical instrument enhances the neuroplasticity and impacts other parts of the brain. It thus has splendid rollover effects.

Read Books:

A plethora of experience and stimuli helps you build lateral connections in your brain. This enables you to nurture your imagination and creativity. You will find a significant improvement in your decision making and executive function.

- **Move Things Around At Home:**

  There is a symbiotic relationship between our bra and environment. The fact is that our physical environment dramatically influences our mental well-being and brain-functions.

Ways to Reset Your Chaotic Brain

You must learn the means to take care of yourself every day. In this process, we forget to regulate the all-important nervous system on which our ability to create, lead, and innovate and live in joy and fun all depend on. In our daily hectic personal and professional life, we are unintentionally and unconsciously placing intense loads on the nervous system. It is high time we pay due attention to tune our nervous system to our growing and changing needs.

1. **Receive The Good.**

   We constantly live in stress, anxiety, and are on high

alert. Psychologists advise us to intentionally stop and overcome this by encoding our brains with the pleasurable feelings of relaxation, calmness, and happiness.

2. Set specific free time slots.

Stick to it always. Then wait and watch. It is life-changing.

3. Interact with friends, family members, and colleagues.

They are your most reliable support system. They keep you grounded in good and bad times.

4. Don't deviate from your schedule.

It helps you in proper time management. You will be saved from the misery of skipping out on essential things. It reduces the mad rush and safeguards you from anxiety.

5. Balance your life.

You feel better and work better. Engaging in diverse activities, unrelated pursuits, and different subject matters is essential. Often the knowledge gained in other subject matters finds its way, cross-pollinates to your primary area of expertise. As long as you're keeping your mind open to new ideas, it will ever get stale.

6. **Segregation of tasks:**

   Segregate or bucket things into two categories: Category 1. Stuff that you can't control, Category 2. Stuff that you can control. Clarity about what you can and what you cannot put concern away. If an item falls into Category 1, you can put it on a work queue to be tackled in time. If an item falls into Category 2, you can attend to it immediately. Reducing uncertainty means reducing anxiety.

Habits for a Healthier Brain and Life

A recent study by Dr. Florian Kurth of UCLA's Department of Neurology showed that from the age of mid to late 20s, your brain begins to wither away and begins to lose some of its functionality. Also, the brain starts to shrink with age. We may not notice this degradation for a long time.

1. **Pay attention to Parasympathetic Wing of Your Nervous System**

   The Parasympathetic nervous system is essential for balanced living and all healing, rebuilding, nourishing, healing, elimination, and regeneration of the body. The parasympathetic nervous system gets stimulated by recreation, relaxation, positive and happy thoughts. All physical and emotional problems are healed by moving and being in a healthy parasympathetic state of mind. It has natural cool-down effects, and you must try to stay there as much of the time as possible. The feeling of lethargy or fatigue makes you relax. The parasympathetic branch is associated with emotional feelings. It is the center of love which drives out fear. Parasympathetic dominance is described as a mental and emotional tendency to remain relaxed or in a parasympathetic state most of the time. You must remain calm and unperturbed at all times.

Learn to activate the Parasympathetic Wing of Your Nervous System

- Rest often.
- Eat well.
- Reduce your stress level as much as possible
- Keep your thoughts and your emotion uplifted and positive.
- Stay in gratitude.
- Practice forgiveness.
- Cultivate contentment.
- Never compare yourself with others.
- Keep negative emotions like worry, fear, anger, and guilt out of your mind.
- Be aware of who and what indeed is the source of your energy.
- Practice deep breathing.

Seven breathing exercises to activate the Parasympathetic Nervous System These exercises induce relaxation and provide several benefits:

Exercise 1:

Take deep breaths. While inhaling air, take care to fill your lungs completely, hold on for a second or two, and then exhale very slowly. Do this for a minute. This relaxed breathing activates the lungs. It also activates the Parasympathetic Nervous System that controls them, giving rest to your body and mind.

Exercise 2:

Relax your body with instant, quick, or deep relaxation techniques. This voluntary and active relaxation helps you to relax even more.

Exercise 3:

Now, we focus on increasing variability of heart rate. Ensure that you breathe so that you inhale and exhale for the same amount of time. For example, you may count numbers one to five for each. All along, imagine that your breath is coming in and out of your heart center of your chest, radiating love, peace, gratitude, and calmness. Incorporate all these positive emotions willfully into your brain. This exercise activates, balances, and harmonizing the variations in a heartbeat, stimulating the parasympathetic nervous system to enhance mental and physical well-being.

Exercise 4:

Be more mindful of physical sensation you feel on your body. Be in a state of total awareness and consciousness. Listen to your breath, to the feeling of your chest, your facial muscles, and the gentle breeze touching your body. This practice of mindful awareness activates the parasympathetic nervous system.

Exercise 5:

Yawning frequently activates the parasympathetic nervous system.

Exercise 6:

Be Focussed on the positive. Feelings like loving-kindness, contentment, tranquility, and gratitude are positive feelings that arouse the parasympathetic nervous system.

Exercise 7:

There is evidence that fiddling with your upper lip increases parasympathetic nervous system activity.

2. Brain Reboot with Deep Relaxation Technique

According to doctors, meditative relaxation has been

associated with reduced stress levels. Though the long-term protective effects of meditation on normal brain atrophy may not be noticed immediately, one may still get many and much quicker short term benefits from meditating.

Eight weeks of meditation bring permanent changes to your brain.

Dr. Eileen Luders and his team did a test on two groups. The first group of 50 meditators and the second group of 50 non-meditators. The meditators showed more brain mass in the scanned images, while the non-meditators showed less brain mass.

A meditation guarantees you a healthier brain and is an excellent reason to make meditation practice a part of your daily routine.

3. The Power of Language "I Choose"

The words you choose are as crucial as your actions. Words don't just convey meaning: they are a force. Words have tremendous power, both to describe and prescribe. You are what you speak.

You communicate your feelings through language. Conscious Language learning is our fundamental software. This operating system supports your thoughts and actions. Your choice of language is very crucial. The language you use can either enhance your ability or hamper your ability to create the experiences of your choice.

THE POWER OF −I

Words speak volumes − to yourself and others − about what you think and how you define yourself. −I know, −I have, I choose, I love, I enjoy, I can, I will, are words of strong and powerful intent. For example, 'Maybe I can,' 'I suppose I can,' are weak expressions and less powerful. −I can't, is a powerful and strong statement of victimization, implying that you have no power to change circumstances outside of your control. The commonly used phrase − I want − rather than bringing you closer tends to distance you from the things you yearn for. −Want reveals a desire which you do not possess. It means you pine for something you accept as being out of our reach. Practice using words like −I choose or −I have instead of −I want and watch the kind of reactions you observe in yourself.

Key ways to adjust your vocabulary and mindset:
- Remember that speaking is a self-fulfilling prophecy. Whatever you speak out verbally,

your mind and body will instantly follow. It becomes your reality – now and in the future continuously.

- Speak in first-person personal.
- Speak about the present: Focus on the present moment, and communicate what you are experiencing right now.
- Let your words be direct and very specific.
- Speak only in the positive.
- Whenever you say the words –I am, the words that follow are compelling, a declaration and these words are received, perceived, and experienced by your subconscious self as a direct order from you as an indication of what you choose to be.

Inner cleansing with Pranayama to utilize breath as a weapon is a science. Prāna, breath, "āyāma," to restrain, and control. Pranayama is the control of the life force. Pranayama is about breathing sequence, the right way of breathing, and mindfulness through breathing.

4. Purification or calming breath techniques

- **Nadi suddhi Pranayama:**

Step 1:

Sit erect in any comfortable posture with eyes closed.

Step 2:

Using your right thumb close your right nostril. Exhale slowly through your left nostril.

Step 3:

Now, inhale slowly and deeply through the same (left) nostril

Step 4:

With the help of your ring finger and your little finger, close the left nostril and release your thumb while you exhale through your right nostril.

Step 5:

Again, breathe in through your right nostril, and then breathe out through your left nostril.

This completes one round of nadi-sudhi.
Repeat 10-20 rounds. It improves concentration, clarity of mind, memory power, IQ, creativity. It is

the strong basic foundation of a superfine structure of spiritual living.

- **Sound Pranayama:**

Your body has its vibratory rate and is easily affected by the sounds around you. You feel good if they are harmonious, and feel irritated if they are discordant. Sound Pranayama arouses and transforms every atom in your physical body, setting up new positive vibrations and conditions, and systematically awakening the sleeping potential and power of the body. Practice Sound Pranayama, which fills you with vigor and strength when you are feeling depressed.

Procedure:

Step 1:

Sit erect in any comfortable posture. Place both your hands in chin mudra on your knees. Keep your eyes closed, face, and shoulders relaxed. Now, inhale deeply and then, loudly vocalize the sound "AH" as you exhale 5-10 times, feeling the divine vibration from the toes to the abdomen.

Step2:

After some rest, now inhale deeply and then repeat, but vocalize the sound "Oo," 5-10 times. Let the vibration permeate slowly and gradually from abdomen, chest and spread down your arms to all your fingers.

Step 3:

Now, inhale deeply and use "MMZ" a humming sound made with closed lips. Feel the vibration started from your throat and extend to your face and head 5-10 times. Rest for a while.

Step 4:

Now, inhale and chant AUM in a single breath The ratio of chanting will be 1:2:3 Feel the divine vibration throughout the body. After completing Sound Pranayama, meditate for 5-15 minutes.

Benefits:
- Sound Pranayama acts as subtle stimulation at the mental level, which can bring in subtle resonance all over the body.
- It is useful in all psychosomatic ailments.
- It bestows peace of mind and illumination.
- It helps to drive away all your worldly

thoughts and reduces distractions.

- When you feel depressed, do this Pranayama, you will be filled with new vigor and strength.

5. Make the Law of Attraction work for you

The Law of Attraction is about Frequency. Like attracts like. It means that a similar frequency attracts each other. Your high frequency attracts the things you want. Your low frequency attracts those things you do not want.

What Lowers Frequency? Anything that makes you feel low and down lowers your frequency.

Intent to control: When you desire to control feelings, yours, and of others, and the outcomes, you are operating out of your wounded self, which naturally lowers your frequency.

Mental distraction: All your senses are outward going. Withdrawal of the senses must be practiced.

Read this story 'The elephant and the fly.'

One day, a Saint and his disciple were walking through a forest. The disciple was restless as his mind was in turmoil and greatly disturbed. He requested his Master to teach him the technique for calming down his mind. The master wanted to teach his disciple with an example. He narrated the story of the elephant and the fly. A hungry elephant was nibbling at the leaves from a high branch of a tree. A small fly came there and was buzzing around its ears. The elephant flapped its large ears to drive it away. However, the adamant fly was moving very close to the elephant with a buzz. Every time, the fly came close to it, and the elephant drove it away with its long ears. The fly got puzzled seeing the elephant unruffled. It was hugely surprising that the elephant remained calm and composed. It asked the elephant how it could stay so cool. The elephant replied, 'I do not allow the five senses to control me. I manage and use my senses as I wish. As you see, I am now eating. My attention is in the process of eating. External factors do not disturb me. So, I am always peaceful.' As long as we are in command of our five senses and can disregard and overcome sense impressions, our power of Manifestation increases in many folds.

6. Pay attention to Color Psychology

Colors affect your brain. It is incredible to know that each color has a unique and specific influence on our brain, our moods, and lifestyle.

- **Red**: It represents love and excitement.
  - Stimulates the neurons and the adrenal gland.
  - Too much exposure causes stress
  - Provokes anger and frustration
  - Stimulates heartbeat and breathing
  - Associated with energy
  - Enhances human metabolism
  - Raised blood pressure

- **Blue**: represents calmness and sadness
  - Has a soothing effect on the human mind.
  - Produces a calming effect
  - Too much exposure causes depression
  - Suppresses appetite
  - Slows human metabolism
  - Materials in blue color appear to be light in weight

- **Yellow**: It represents warmth and energy
  - Helps to release Serotonin, causing a happy mood.
  - Too much exposure causes fatigue
  - Speeds up metabolism
  - Babies cry more in yellow rooms
  - Evokes pleasant, cheerful feelings.

- **Purple** represents wealth, mystery, wisdom
  - Develop spirituality and deep thoughts
  - Causes frustration
  - Evokes gloom and sad feeling

- **Gray,** It unsettles you
  - Creates expectations

- **White,** It represents purity and innocence
  - Has a calming effect
  - Represents a successful beginning

- **Green** represents envy
  - Relaxes the body and alleviates stress
  - Has a soothing effect on the eyes
  - Improves vision

- Has a healing and hygienic effect

- **Orange** represents enthusiasm and attention
  - Increases oxygen supply to the brain
  - Stimulates mental abilities
  - Increases appetite
  - Increases mental activities

- **Pink** represents romance and kindness
  - Reduces anger and anxiety
  - Denotes feminine qualities

- **Black,** It represents evil and unhappiness
  - Gives the feeling of perspective and depth
  - Makes people wearing it look thinner.

- **Brown** represents reliability and strength.
- Enter the fantastic world of colors and choose the right color to boost your brain health.

Ways To Start Fresh to Keep Your Brain Fit

Your brain is the most essential tool you have. You are using only a tiny percent of this amazing engineering machine's capacity. Just as you cannot climb a mountain without a fit body, you cannot redesign your life without resetting your brain.

A rebirth, a restart

1. **Accept Change**

    Change is inevitable, and a natural process in this Universe. It may be hard in the beginning, but soon, everything will fall into place again.

2. **Accept Defeat**

    Though it hurts badly, accept defeat and move on. Come out of the comfort zone.

3. **Make Peace With The Past**

    Write Down The Worst-Case Scenario. This reveals that it is much easier than you feel.

4. **Clean Up Your Closet, room, house**

    Throw away the clothes, devices, things, and memories that drag you down. The more you let go of things, the more light you will feel. This way, you move more comfortably and faster. The change appears like a natural path, not an effort.

5. **Limit The Stuff You Own**

Let the notion of simple living and high thinking guide your journey of life. Get rid of all your unnecessary possessions. You have better things to do than just managing your stuff.

6. Your Hard-disk needs a Format

Your brain is like a computer-hard disc, which needs a quick format now and then does a raw format. Purposefully re-arrange all contents in your brain, and destroying some of your hard-disk sectors. Re-engineer your social life at its deepest level. It is your makeover from your obsolete, old you. It is a cleansing process. It helps you move forward to be functional again.

7. Break Up An Old Habit

It is said, habits die hard. By shifting some of your small, unconscious behaviors, you can ignite a more significant change in your life. It is metamorphosis at work.

8. Create A New Habit

Monotony enters your life when you start leading your life like a machine, on auto-pilot mode. You must break an old habit of yours consciously choosing a new habit now.

9. Practice Your "Yes" and Practice Your "No" Too

Any positive growth and change will be fueled by your capacity to say 'Yes' to the right things. Also, learn how to say an affirmative 'No' to things that hamper your growth. You have the power to say "Yes" to the present, and "No" to the past.

These great exercises not only enhance your creativity but also strengthen your change muscles. It builds up your courage to take action. You will be more aware of and receptive to spot new opportunities and broaden your vision.

10.   Wipe Your Glasses

Though the road to change is right in front of you, you fail to see it because you are blurred. I mean, your life glasses are blurred. Your brain is like a camera which doesn't know how and where to focus. You need to move it back and forth a few times and see what picture it shows. In the end, it is you who must decide what picture to click with the camera.

11. Do Act. Don't React

You must train your brain to respond to the external stimuli and never to react or overreact. If you are reacting to what is happening around you, then peace will always elude you. Reacting to the financial crisis, social rejection, etc. only increases your fear and anxiety. It is only when you are calm and composed that you make the right judgment and the right decision. Always remember, That too shall pass.

12. Shift Your Focus

A Focus shift is all that you need for a new

beginning. We are the creators of our destiny. What we focus on, grows. Our focus generates our reality. Though this is easier said than done, you can do it. So, start training.

13. Stop Solving The Wrong Problem

Do not attach too much importance to what others say about you and to their opinion. Introspect and if you find merit in their views, take it. Otherwise, leave it. Do we think of a thing after we throw it into the trash can? Use your brain for the right things, which adds value to your life. Stay sharp and cool.

14. Forget "I Can," Embrace "I Do"

Change your monologue. There is a world of difference between 'I can' and 'I do.' Many research studies have shown that you are, to a great extent, what you think about yourself and what you are saying to yourself. Words have meaning. The phrase "I Can," is no doubt, empowering but "I Do" is life changing. You will be amazed by the results this brings to your life. This kindles and sparks a new beginning for you.

15. Pamper yourself with A Long Distance Trip

Traveling great distances is thoroughly enjoyable and also very rewarding. It changes something inside you. It bestows you with a new perspective, creative, and innovative ideas. Something fresh and surprising always emerges from a trip. Take time off for yourself. Do not be imprisoned forever in your never-ending work routine. Take a break. You'll be back, more energetic, a new enthusiastic person.

16. Stop Trying To Be Perfect

The biggest mind trap is perfection. It restrains you from enjoying your precious present moments. Perfection signifies you have reached the end of the journey. You must always strive to be better instead, most importantly, a better human being. This gives you the necessary room for change and improvement.

17. Eliminate Self Sabotage

Overcome the self-sabotage mindset that prevents you from growing. You are, in fact, your best friend and also your worst enemy. It is the fear of failure, which stops you from pursuing your cherished dreams. With the right mindset, you can make the impossible possible.

18. Rechannel Aggression

It helps you. Aggressiveness is not toxic; you use it in the right channel and direction. So, intentionally re-channel this huge force, this immense energy flowing in you, and put it to productive work. Don't bottle it deep down. It may harm you. Let it out by channeling it in the right direction. Your life will certainly change for the better after this shift and reconnection. By shifting your perspective, you'll start to understand which parts of you are the same, and which ones are changed.

A rebirth and a restart with Brain Reset

A. Acupuncture and Brain Reset

Acupuncture, Traditional Chinese Medicine, is an excellent alternative to good mental health and for relief from stress and anxiety. With Acupuncture therapy, the brain releases neuropeptides. It helps the brain release the brain's natural pain killers endorphins that help your brain produce more of these essential chemicals. Acupuncture improves blood flow throughout your body as it constricts blood vessels, and release vasodilators, which causes your blood vessels to relax. This reduces both cerebral blood pressure and high blood pressure in your body. It helps correct various autonomic nerve-related disorders like epilepsy, cardiovascular diseases, anxiety and nervousness, depression, etc. Recent studies concluded that acupuncture alters neurotransmitters in your brain, and alleviates symptoms of nerve-related disorders and stop your autonomic response. It thus has a positive impact on your mental wellness. Acupuncture therapy can soothe your brain's response to stress as it activates the parasympathetic nervous system. The heart rate slows down, blood pressure, and cortisol levels drop.

B. Biofeedback

Biofeedback is a way to retrain your brain waves. It is the scientific technique to manipulate and change your biological state by consciously trying to change it through visualizations. An ECG biofeedback, also known as Brain biofeedback, is the neurofeedback that helps to reset or regulate your brain waves. In this treatment procedure, a few sensors are placed on the head, which captures the power and frequency of the brain's electrical activity. Therapists track the five brain waves, namely the delta, theta, alpha, beta, and gamma waves on a computer. The brainwaves captured by the biofeedback device will be seen on a computer screen. They repeatedly send this information back to the brain using an electrical signal or computer imagery.

C. Acupressure and Brain Mapping

In Acupressure, practitioners apply pressure to acupoints on the body meridians using their fingers, palms, elbows, feet, or special devices. *Acupressure* is found to be very useful to improve memory, balancing the *Brain* Chemistry, and brain Recovery.

A 3-Minute Acupressure Routine can help clear your Brain Fog, which is slower-than-usual thinking. Along with changes in your diet, this 3-minute acupressure technique can help stimulate, excite, and clear up your brain fog instantly. You must try to stimulate each of those acupressure points for at least 60 to 90 seconds applying moderate pressure. Do two to three cycles. Acupressure moves chi (energy) and oxygenates and gets the brain juices flowing again. This clears your mind.

These three acupressure hot spots clear up your mind and help fight brain fog:

1. Si Shen Cong, the 4 Extraordinary Points on the top of your head.

2. DU20, located at the vertex of your head.

3. KI 1, or Kidney 1 are located on the bottom of your foot.

Important Acupressure Reflex points that improve concentration and memory power:

- Heavenly Pillar

- Third Eye Point

- Bigger Rushing

- Three Mile Point

- Middle of a Person

- Gates of Consciousness

- Effective Brain Point

The Acupressure technique helps your brain to relax and improves your concentration power. You will have a happy and healthy brain.

Conclusion

Everything is created twice. First, in your mind and then in the outside world. Realize that now, in this very moment, you are creating your life. You are creating your next moment. So, let your mind create what is the best for you.

Life is like riding a bicycle. You must keep on moving to keep your balance.

Watch Your WATCH: You must always watch your

Words

Actions

Thoughts

Character and

Habits.

You must learn unique and novel ways to think before you can master a new way of living. The first crucial step towards getting somewhere is to decide emphatically that you are not going to stay where you are at present. The old skin has to be shed before the new one can come. You must renew, change, rejuvenate yourself; otherwise, you will go stale.

You must change for the better. It is only by making small and consistent changes in your daily routine that you will change your life. Your success lies in your daily routine. Our daily habits and decisions impact our brain health, success, and happiness.

Say Yes to 3 A's: Accept, Adjust, and Appreciate.

Say No to the 3 C's: Never Criticize, Condemn, or Complain

Go on. Do not halt. Do not stagnate. Rest not.

Stagnation, procrastination and falling into old routines nurture destruction which overpowers creation.

You must never choose inaction.

Be the change agent. Create a transformational relationship, Add value to every moment. Add value to every relation. Be an alchemist. In helping others to become better, you become better. Lead the way. Be a change agent. Strive, and Keep going.

www.ingramcontent.com/pod-product-compliance
Lightning Source LLC
Chambersburg PA
CBHW051346280526
45784CB00007B/2841